Uluru
Journey

An exploration into
narrative theology

Denham Grierson

The Joint Board of Christian Education
Melbourne

Published by
THE JOINT BOARD OF CHRISTIAN EDUCATION
65 Oxford Street, Collingwood 3066, Australia

ULURU JOURNEY
© Denham Grierson 1996

National Library of Australia
  Cataloguing-in-Publication entry.

Grierson, Denham
Uluru Journey: an exploration into narrative theology

Bibliography
ISBN: 1 86407 122 2.

1. Christian pilgrims and pilgrimages - Northern Territory - Ayers Rock. 2. Storytelling - Religious aspects - Christianity. 3. Narrative (Rhetoric). 4. Ayers Rock (N.T.) I. Joint Board of Christian Education. II. Title.

248.4630994291

First printed 1996

Cover photograph by Coo-ee Picture Library
Cover design by Kelvin
Design by Robina Norton
Typeset by MacTop in Janson 10/11
Printed by Shortrun Books

JB96/3698

'If my faith leads me to create life or to increase it, what further proof of my faith would you have?'

Miguel de Unamuno

Table of Contents

Acknowledgements

The manuscript of this book was written during six months of study leave given to me by the Victorian Council of Christian Education. I have profited from visits to Bali as a guest of the Protestant Church of Bali, conversations with the staff and students of Nungalinya College in Darwin and survivors of the Holocaust at the Holocaust Museum in Melbourne.

I have been helped by suggestions on the text from Doug and Maisie McKenzie, and by Gail Wager and Gleda Didsbury who at different times helped with typing. My son, Peter, gave generously of his time in taming the computer and to my wife, Mavis, as always, my thanks are due for her support. Much of the material has been shared with students of the United Faculty of Theology over several years.

To the VCCE and all those who have contributed to the book in any way I express my thanks. It has been a task of passing on what has been given to me with the hope that it may bring more life and light to all who read its pages.

The author and publishers gratefully acknowledge financial assistance towards the publication of this book from the Florence Wagstaff bequest, administered by the Senatus of the Uniting Church Theological Hall, Melbourne; and from the Victorian Council of Christian Education.

Introduction

At the beginning it had no name. Its first name was Uluru, given to it by the inhabitants of the Western Desert countless centuries ago. In recent time, it was called by another generation, Ayers Rock. To ordinary Australians, it is simply The Rock.

Uluru Journey

Chapter 1

The Sentinel

Uluru is approached across a vast inland sea, now reduced to wind swept desert. So flat is the land that coming from one direction and looking across the red sand-dunes of the Western Desert, Ayers Rock can be seen 150 kilometres in the distance. Coming from another direction and upon cresting a ridge, suddenly there the Rock stands, dominating, impressive and still 100 kilometres away. Tourist brochures state that it is 'the very heart of Australia'.

The time of Ayers Rock

In 1872, Ernest Giles, as his expedition crossed the desert, recorded seeing The Rock but did not name it. It was named Ayers Rock in 1873 by William Christie Gosse after Sir Henry Ayers, who was a Premier of South Australia. So, a white explorer, newly come to the ancient land we call Australia, 'discovered' the huge monolith. Naming the rock secured it as a white possession. That was the way of it in those days.

Geologists were to follow, who described the Rock their way:

> … it was originally laid down as horizontal sandstone
> bedding from weathered granites out of which the mica was
> bleached to form an arkose rock containing plagioclase
> felspar and a microcline quartz. Its present tilted position
> was caused by upheavals in Protozoic times when the great
> Centralian fault lines occurred and formed the folding that
> can be observed in the mountain ranges around Alice
> Springs. [1]

A more expansive description can be constructed easily.
Ayers Rock is a rounded monolith 2570 metres long from east to west and 1500 metres tall. The origins of this arresting geological

phenomenon go back 600 million years, and to the junction of pre-Cambrian and Cambrian times. There are other such structures on other continents but none as massive, as mysterious, as solitary. Eons have passed since its earliest beginnings, countless times of heat and cold, gigantic stresses and eruptions, times of flood and times of wind-swept aridity. Forty million years ago, a long process of erosion began, sweeping away the surrounding molasse so that gradually the contours and shape of Ayers Rock began to appear from the flat plains that ran away in every direction. Something like its present form emerged. Uluru stood silent, waiting.

The time of Uluru

Perhaps 30,000 years ago, some say 40,000, others 60,000, the first Aborigines came to the Rock. They had their own story of how the Rock came into being, at the time of creation, of the sacred dreaming.[2] Then no humans were present, only the ancestral creator spirits who roamed across the undifferentiated face of the continent. It was the beginning of time, when the features of the landscape were created, when patterns of relationship were established and the sacred cycles laid down that would shape and guide all that was to come. Out of this primordial beginning, the inter-relatedness of land, law and people, was set forever. The land itself spoke of spirit presence and intentionality.

In that primal time - before time - the Rock was the site of much activity. Creator spirits lived, fought, created, and celebrated, cross-hatching the Rock with story and myth, their titanic struggles leaving visible signs in the rock-face for generations today to look upon and wonder.

This Rock was sacred place, filled with spirit presence, powerful with Law. It spoke to the people who, over time, came to live there and know its story.

In this story, secret, arcane, was the connection between that time and now. The very plan of life itself was carried in the communication of that Dreaming time. So the events associated with these myths, told around the camp fires to the young, of the ritual practices, patterns of behaviour, social habits and responsibilities, gave strength and authority to the design of life that the creator spirits of the Dreaming had laid down. The supernatural beings that 'had been born out of their own eternity', still were present although under the ground, or now in the shape of rocks, trees or tjurunga objects, returned to their first state of sleep. At Uluru, the sacred Wanambi serpent, which lives in the rock hole of Uluru, watches over the totemic ancestors and the people.

So the Pitjantjatjara and Yankuntjatjara people believed. For they were the people of Uluru and the land of the Western Desert. So it is also for the people of Mutitjulu, the community that lives at the Rock today. Beneath the surface, the creator spirits rest, still alive and active, responsive to the ceremonies and rituals which ensure a true creation and a continuing care and responsibility for the land.

The time which is now

In 1985, when the land surrounding Uluru was returned to Aboriginal people, an agreement was reached to allow tourists to continue to climb the Rock as they had done like an increasing stream of ants since William Gosse and his camel driver first climbed it in 1873. Tour operators and promoters of the tourist industry feared that tourists would cease to come to the Rock if the climb was forbidden. The climb was a feature of publicity at home and abroad. Successful climbers proudly wear tee-shirts which proclaim 'I climbed Ayers Rock'. The Aboriginal community agreed reluctantly to accept this invasion of the sacred area. It is today the practice of many tourists to climb Ayers Rock. Uluru, which is another place in another time and mystic frame, is not real for them, for like all white fellas, they have no dreaming.

The Rock, Ayers Rock, Uluru, means many things to many people. It is a symbol of extraordinary power, a symbol deep in the national consciousness of Australians who know and puzzle at this singularity at the very heart of the continent: the largest monolith in the world, situated so dramatically in vast desert plains that its true size cannot be properly discerned. Nor understood. Is it fanciful under the Tropic of Capricorn to call up the story of *The Sentinel* to set imagination aflame. In Arthur Clarke's short story, made into the film, *2001 A Space Odyssey*, a slab is found on the far side of the moon, that points humankind to its destiny. Mysterious, unique, evocative, the slab sends a signal into space, a trajectory along which humankind must seek a future.

In the Western Desert, Uluru stands, as it has for millions upon millions of years. This giant singularity stands alone, mysterious, unique, evocative, pointing to what? For Uluru means many things to many people. It waits for visitors and receives them all. Most are tourists. A few are pilgrims.

Chapter 2

Nipper Kamari

Rain was falling steadily, the sound of it easily heard on the roof by the eight people gathered in the living room of one of the Emu Walk apartments. Situated in the town of Yulara, built near Ayers Rock to a design by the company of Phillip Cox and Associates, several Emu Walk apartments had been booked by Pilgrim Tours for two nights for its present tour group. Although it was 9 o'clock in the morning, the light struggling through the cloud cover was not strong.

Alan Vizard, tour guide and proprietor of Pilgrim Tours, spread his hands in apology: 'Usually the rainfall in the desert around here is about 230 to 260 mm a year. We seem to have arrived on the day they got the lot in one go!' No one made any comment, although their faces revealed their disappointment. Vizard continued, 'As you know, we were to explore the Rock today with Nipper Kamari as guide, but there is no chance with this rain. So Nipper will be here shortly to talk to us about the area and Aboriginal beliefs. He shouldn't be long'.

Vizard watched the company as they began chatting to each other. Two weeks on the road together had given him an insight into his charges. He remembered the first briefing in Melbourne three weeks ago, the air of anticipation, his attempts to explain the philosophy of Pilgrim Tours.

They must have speculated about him, as he told them his story. At the age of 35, restless and dissatisfied with teaching literature and Australian history in a state secondary school in Yarraville, he had resigned. At least, that was the official explanation. At that time, his own mid-life crisis bearing down on him, he had decided to explore the Australian continent. His background in history and Australian literature gave him a thorough grounding so the concept of Pilgrim Tours developed. He had long been a devotee of Chaucer, so the choice of the name 'Pilgrim Tours' seemed inevitable. [3]

Pilgrim Tours

The first publicity brochure proclaimed 'Pilgrim Tours - Something Different. Join others like yourself who wish to explore Australia and its spiritual heritage. Visit sacred sites. Talk with Aboriginal people. Listen to the stories of outback Australians. Visit the Old Timers at Alice Springs. Call at Uluru and Kata Tjura to hear the myths of the Dream Time. And much more. DISCOVER AUSTRALIA. Here is a pilgrimage that matters'.

His photograph flattered him, he thought. Premature greying hair, blue eyes that seemed humorous even on paper, a tall spare figure that made him appear as a proto-typical bushman. Even his broken nose, beneath the bush hat pushed well back on his head, added veracity to the image of a seasoned outback guide.

'Niche marketing', his adviser at the Small Business Council had called it. The purchase of the twelve seater, air-conditioned mini bus, specially equipped for outback travel, had sealed the decision. He was committed. He had hoped that others like himself, who were on a peculiarly Australian quest for identity and meaning, would join each four-week tour.

Three years had taught him how idealistic he had been. He had learned the hard way how difficult it is to live harmoniously with a group of assorted human beings, all with variant agendas and divergent expectations. Like the retired executive who had brought a metal detector along and insisted on looking for gold at every stop, to the increasing frustration of everyone else. The outcome was inevitable. One morning, the detector was missing. It was found some days later by the side of the road, crumpled and unusable.

Still he had prospered. Contacts had been built up. Word of mouth had kept his numbers high. He had made a slight profit on the second year's tours. He was content. But in his heart he knew he was still searching. He came back again and again to the question: 'If Australians were to go on pilgrimage in Australia to confirm or discover a twentieth century religious identity, where would they go?' His present tour group to his eye was the closest to what he had hoped for when he first began. He quickly reviewed what he knew of them.

The travellers identified

To his left sat Jane Orchard, the youngest of the group at twenty-four. A short, intelligent young women, with close-cropped black hair, Jane, he had learned some days ago, was a researcher with a book publishing company, engaged to be married next year and searching for some certainty about making such a life-long commitment. 'I am', she said in a moment of frankness, 'running away to sort things out'. There was an honesty about her that Vizard found slightly disconcerting.

Jane Orchard was talking to Daniel Levi, who sat next to her. At the first introductions weeks ago, Daniel had growled, 'Daniel Levi, Jewish, thirty-six years of age, graphic designer and state of the art neurotic'. He wasn't neurotic, thought Vizard, a little confused perhaps, earnest and ironic. The slightly built Levi with his self-deprecating remarks had been an asset to the group. 'I am after', Levi had announced, 'a kind of understanding. Why was I born Jewish and not you?' He was hard to dislike. The edge of suffering beneath the public persona was visible to all.

Helen Wales was next. 'Wales are a dying breed', she had joked, 'whether in the water or the banking business.' They had all laughed, appreciating the warmth and openness that came from her every movement. 'I am taking a break from the family business, textiles and marketing' (this with a wry face) 'my father's business, not my husband's, who lives elsewhere these last seven years doing his usual "marketing" without me.' Despite her approachability, there was a distance in her, a country not open to strangers. Of all the travellers, Helen seemed most abstracted. Many times she had sought her own company. Vizard concluded 'there is a mystery here', but at fifty-four years of age, what person did not nurture many mysteries known only to their own heart?

Ian Standfast leaned over to offer Helen a biscuit from the coffee table between them. At sixty-six, the retired Uniting Church clergyman had been a complete surprise. On first acquaintance, Vizard had judged him imperious and almost certainly pious. But first impressions in this case had been wrong. Perhaps it was shyness that made the balding, stout cleric seem autocratic in manner, with his ruddy complexion and habit of folding his hands across a generous waistline.

Upon further acquaintance, Vizard had found a fellow traveller in every sense. Standfast was inquiring, with an intellect that emerged more formidably from every conversation. Not that Ian sought to display his knowledge. He had proved an excellent listener and Vizard had shared his own heart's desire with Standfast on more than one occasion. Vizard, watching him, found the line from Chaucer coming to mind 'That if gold rust, what then will iron do?'.[4]

Standfast had told them he was a widower. He had, in response to why he was on the tour, offered an obtuse explanation. 'I have always wondered what the answer to Jesus' question was - What did you go out into the desert to see? He had chuckled and added: 'Vizard, I expect my money's worth!!'

Two of the remaining members of the group were reading details of the facilities available in the Emu Walk apartments. Lila Sedura was a tall Indonesian exchange student with a ready and attractive smile. Married four years ago, Lila had spent the last two years as a student completing a Master's degree at RMIT in information technology. 'On my return to Bali', she told them, 'I will be employed by a hotel chain in overseeing their computer systems.'

Her reasons for taking the trip at first had seemed mundane. 'To learn a little about Australia and improve my English - particularly idiomatic English'. This latter comment had produced a ripple of comment and advice from Levi that it would probably be so idiomatic that it could not be used in public company. Lila had explained subsequently that for her, the return to Bali presented many difficulties. 'To live in two cultures with different roles and expectations of women is very confusing. I hope to learn a little on how to re-enter my own culture from encounters with first Australians.'

Colin Freeman was the least known of the group to Vizard. Not that Freeman was unfriendly or non-communicative. The solidly built, thirty year old had readily shared that he was a scientist working currently on a government project, investigating the long-term effects of fluoro-carbons on the ozone layer. 'A waste of time really', he had added. 'The politicians don't want to know.'

But it was hard to get at the centre of Colin's concerns. When asked why he had joined Pilgrim Tours, he had responded, 'I have fallen off the edge of scientific certainties and out of the wreck of humanism'. No-one had the courage to ask him what he meant. It would have been easier thought, Vizard, if he had said 'to have a wow of a time'.

The last member of the group, Archie Marshall, was, as Vizard focused on him, characteristically in motion. Archie was never still. His diminutive figure was always to hand, offering food, giving advice, telling jokes, helping with the luggage. Archie was a doer. Vizard looked at him with affection, for he understood Archie very well. A lad from the northern suburbs, filled with anecdotes, and the possessor of an extraordinary array of practical skills, Archie, now in his forties, was the life of the party. His red knitted hat, rarely off his head, flitted around the group, giving the others the sense of being mothered by an aging robin red breast, as Colin put it.

Archie had, at their orientation gathering, compared himself to the chicken who, instead of crossing the road, laid her eggs in the middle - because she wanted to lay it on the line. 'I am', he said, 'on holiday. Take it or leave it. A grim pill I am not.' But no one took offence. No one ever did with Archie. They knew he would rather cause a laugh than have a feed, They also saw in the wrinkled brown face, honesty and integrity. In the end, you could count on Archie. He was trusted by them all.

Vizard ticked the company off in his mind: Jane Orchard, Daniel Levi, Helen Wales, Ian Steadfast, Lila Sedura, Colin Freeman, Archie Marshall and himself. A smaller group than usual. Each on a pilgrimage for their own reasons. Outside, the wind had picked up in intensity. Sudden storms over Yulara and Uluru were not uncommon but usually short-lived. It was the restriction the rain caused which worried Alan Vizard.

The Rock was the centrepiece of their tour. For him it had always a mysterious fascination and evoked feelings he could not name nor adequately explain to himself. Yet since their arrival, cloud and rain had obscured the Rock. Lightning flashes broke out over the plains. Visibility was negligible. 'We shall have to spend today indoors at this rate. No-one can drive in that lot!' Then 'I hope Nipper comes soon!'

Thinking of Nipper Kamari brought a flood of genuine pleasure. Nipper was a typical representative of his people. About five foot four inches in height, dark long hair, soft brown eyes with a flat squashed nose, Nipper had been a ranger in the National Park for six years. His knowledge of desert lore was impressive, his understanding of Aboriginal dreaming myths comprehensive.

Vizard had first met Nipper when he was telling a group of international tourists a most improbable story about a goanna and a hare wallaby. Nipper had glanced across, saw Vizard's grin, took in his bush gear and knew the game was up. Afterwards, the two had shared a drink at the Desert Gardens Hotel and so began a firm friendship. Nipper had introduced Alan to his wife and five children with a typical comment: 'This fella Nipper has real trouble'. Alan recognised how deeply the Kamari family loved each other from that first simple remark.

The Dreaming

'Nipper is on Territory time again.' Alan glanced at his watch and decided to begin anyway. Nipper would come in his own good time. 'I think we will begin', said Vizard. Upon his word, people found chairs and quickly fell silent as he began to speak.

When Nipper arrives he will tell you a little of the world view of Aboriginal people. The religion of Aboriginal Australians is subtle and complex, at once mystical and intensely practical. Their mythic world binds together cosmological, religious, sociological and psychological dimensions into one unbroken whole. It is certain that what we are told is only a part of a rich complex body of knowledge. We are told what is public knowledge. There is secret knowledge which only the Elders have. That is why it is dangerous to generalise about what we hear. Stories about the same series of events vary from group to group. Details are occasionally at variance. Our capacity to hear truly is not highly developed. In any case we are being told only what it is safe to know.

Vizard shifted in his chair and glanced around the room. 'In Aboriginal thought there are three unchanging realities. The Law, given at the time of the Dreaming, which cannot be varied or broken. The Land, to which the people have a continuing relationship and ritual responsibility, and the People, who are interrelated by totemic association, a profound connectedness which relates person to person, defines marriage groups and outlines ritual patterns across the whole of the continent.

Something of the force of this can be illustrated by comparing how different cultures greet each other. In the West we say 'How are you?'. The question is important because, in a variable climate, concern for health is realistic. Flu and colds affect us at all times of the year.

In Indonesia, the greeting is 'Where are you going?' The comment arises from a trader economy where the price of rice was of daily concern. Someone going in a particular direction might indicate a change in the rice price. Also in a dangerous environment, it enabled people to warn each other of dangers to be met in a particular direction. It helped people know where loved ones could be found in an emergency.

Kalahari bushmen, who are very small, greet each other with the words 'I saw you coming from afar!' suggesting importance and significance. With Aborigines the question is, 'What is your name?' By discovering the totem of a person, you know how you are to relate to each other, whether you can talk, be associated or share communal activity together. All relationships are governed by one's totem group or name.

To return to the land for a moment, you will be familiar perhaps with the book *The Songlines*. [5] In that book, the author attempts to understand how the lines of the passage of creator spirits in the Dreaming criss-cross Australia. Each tribal group knows the songs which belong to them. They form part of a song cycle that covers the Continent. Each group, on appropriate ceremonial occasions, must sing their song, precisely as it was handed down, and in proper sequence.

The songs of the Dreaming therefore recreate the earth, for they repeat again the song of the first ancestor beings that gave form and shape to the Australian landscape. Trees, rocks, ranges, waterholes, all these are held in being by the true rendition of the Song cycles. To break the cycle, to sing it out of sequence, to forget it, is to bring deep trouble upon the land and people. The songs and ceremonies go on creating the land.

The relationship with the land is intimate. 'How can we be well when the land is sick?' they say. By which is meant, if the mother is ill how can the children not suffer. Since the relationship between law, land and people is so intimately connected, one cannot be separated from another. Identity is bound up with proper respect for all that is seen.

Uluru is at the crossroads of a series of songlines, a network of dreaming tracks which are the routes taken by ancestral heroes. Traditional Aboriginal law requires a proper care of sacred sites. It is the responsibility of each tribal group to protect the dreaming places and to remember and enact through song, stories and ceremonies, the great deeds from the beginning of time.

When the Dreaming began

While white people can only guess at what this kind of identification with the land means, it is sometimes possible to get a sense of it through a story. Jim Poulter wrote a story for children called *The Secret of Dreaming*, which goes like this in broad detail: [6]

> Once, only the Spirit of All Life existed. Then in the mind of the Creator Spirit a dreaming began. First a Dreaming of Fire grew, then a Dreaming of Wind, and a Dreaming of Rain. Fire, Wind and Rain, in the Dreaming which did not stop but continued.
> A Dreaming of Earth, Sky, Land and Sea followed, and the Dreaming continued. Life was sent into the Dreaming.
> First in the spirit of Barramundi. Barramundi dreamed in the deep still waters, but Barramundi did not understand the Dream.
> It passed to Currikee, the Turtle, who dreamed in the rocks and sun, but Currikee did not understand the Dream.
> Nor Bogei the Lizard, who passed it on to Bunjil the Eagle. Bunjil rose in the sky and began the dream, but only of the wind and open sky. The spirit of Goonerang the Possum then took the Dream, but Goonerang did not understand it, wanting only trees and night sky. The spirit of Kangaroo took the Dream among the plain of yellow grass, a dream of music, song and laughter. Kangaroo understood it not at all.
> So the Dream passed on to the Spirit of Man, who saw all the works of creation, and heard the songs of birds, and saw sunset, and listened also in the Dreaming for the laughter of

children. And Man understood the Dream. And all things
that had been dreamed before. And that all creatures were
his spirit cousins, and that he must protect the Dreaming.
He dreamed how to tell these secrets to his unborn child.
The Great Spirit knew then that the secret of the Dreaming
was safe. Tired out from dreaming Creation, the Spirit of
Life sank into the ground, there to rest. As do the spirits of
all creatures when they become tired. They join the Spirit of
Life in the Land. So this is why the Land is sacred. This is
why we must be its caretaker.

While such a story constructs an imaginative process that is helpful
to us, it does not claim to be true as Aboriginal story is true. At least
not in detail. What it does is demonstrate the mythic unity of all
created things. That is why it is hard to accept any mining company's
action that despoils a sacred site without reference either to Australian
law or Aboriginal tradition, as if it does not matter. For such a company
a fine of $5,000 is nothing. For the Aborigines it is an unspeakable
sacrilege. From their point of view they have failed to protect the
Dreaming. Bad things will happen.

It was at this point that Nipper Kamari arrived, bringing with him
into the room the smell of damp and smoke and the odour of outdoor
living. After suitable introductions and a period of settling down, he
was asked to speak to the group. Following some general introductory
comments, as he summed up the group, Nipper, with a hesitant smile,
began to talk about his people.

The Law, the Land, the People

Aboriginal people know that our story is in the land. I don't know
how many thousand years my people walked this land. I reckon maybe
60,000 years. I can't say when it began. No-one can. But it was a
sacred time. It was the time of the Dreaming. Then powerful story
happened. That story is told to me by my father. His father told him.
And I tell my children. My children get to keep this story close. That
story never changes. The Law never changes.

I tell you why the law never changes. Because each one has his
place, his own country... where to stand. You can't take your country
with you, so always you come back to your country. And your story.
And the law. You understand what I say to you. Aboriginal law never
changes. It is always the same. You got to keep it, otherwise no-one
walks in the right way.

See, it is to keep alive, we follow the Law. If we waste today, next
year we can't get enough food. Because we did not care and we get

trouble. How can we survive if we forget the story? If we have no dreaming?

White people have no dreaming. They don't listen to us when we say this is powerful story. Trouble come if you forget the story. They only listen for money... money.

The sacred places speak to us. The land is our story. And the story is kept in the sacred places. And the sacred objects. That is why we look after these places and our children will also. That's the law.

The Dreaming place like Uluru. You can't change it. I can't change it. No matter whether you King, or Prime Minister, or rich man, or important bloke, it is the way it is. That is secret Dreaming place. You cannot go there because this is powerful place, and we frightened you get hurt if you go there. Uninitiated, can't go there. Only death come to those who don't listen.'

Nipper Kamari is aware that his words are having an effect and he becomes more passionate.

'This land is like your mother and father. You come from this place and you go back to this place. When you die you go back under the earth. This earth is like brother and sister. And the song we sing, and dance, that song keeps the land whole. This is true story I tell you. It can't change. It is law that we are responsible to love the land and to keep the secret things and to do the Law. It won't move. That is why you must have this story.

For man cannot split himself. Clothes can change. Language can change. Transport can change. But each one must remain true to his story and his land and his people. My grandfather told me this. And his grandfather told him. And I tell my children 'If you lose your story you lose yourself'. We live in story as the fish live in water. Without our story we have no life. Once the Dreaming is lost, the end is near.[7]

Jane Orchard put up her hand. 'Could you share a little of that story with us Nipper? I mean, if you are allowed to...' A mischievous glint appeared in Nipper's eyes for a moment, but a swift glance from Vizard checked his impulse to stir the possum. Nipper nodded and continued:

At the dawn of time, in the Dreamtime, the ancestor spirits began to move. When you dream, you dream things. Trees, animals, springs. They move in your feeling. Fleeting shapes come. We remember the time. The time before time when the ancestor spirits came out of the ground. They gave shape to the land. From their deeds all things were born. All that you see around here. All of it is sacred Dream time.

Then the creator fellas moved across the land. The giant Rainbow snake, the Earth mother, the totem ancestors. The bull roarers spoke the work of creation. Our great Earth mother giving birth. These paths along which the Dream time spirits moved are ways of power, powerful ways. Our people know this.

Uluru Dreaming

I tell you some of those stories about Uluru. Once in the beginning, in the Dream time, Uluru was the home place of a great Wanambi: a many coloured snake, bigger than the rainbow. That Wanambi has no song. That one is forever. He still lives in Uluru for he always stay by the waterhole. He lives in caverns beneath the pool that is still there. If you want to drink, first light a fire for that Dreaming One is jealous of that place. He kill those who disturb his sleeping.

In the time of creation, the Kunia (carpet snake) people came to Uluru from the West. They made their camps beside the waterhole, on the south side of it. They hunted, gathered food and sang. Everywhere today you see the marks they left. Some boulders you see are Kunia people. Grass tufts are the pubic hair of the women.

Well, near the Kunia camp, the sleepy lizard man, Meta-lungana was staying. He was mean and selfish. He kept all he had to himself. When he kill emu, he would not bring it home until dark. So he did not have to share it. One time, while Meta-lungana was cooking a kalaia (emu) he had just killed, he saw smoke rising in the southern land of Djira. He quickly hid his emu meat, knowing that strangers were coming his way.

The strangers, as was the custom, told the lizard man they had hunted emu but in vain. They were hungry. Then they waited for the offer of food. Meta-lungana said nothing. They spoke again of the hunt and their need. But still Meta-lungana made no offer of food. Then the wind brought the smell of cooked meat to their nostrils. Angry at the deceit and the breaking of the custom of hospitality, they took a burning stick from the cooking fire and set the grass and dry leaves of the shelter protecting Meta-lungana alight. There was no escape. Smoke overcame the lizard man. He did not know where to run. He died in agony in the fire. Even now you look at the sleepy lizard and see the marks of the fire upon him. Even now he moves slowly and painfully. So it is for all time.

That story is written on Uluru. The Metjan Gorge marks the place of Meta-lungana's camp. If you look up from there you see the black lines where he dragged the emu from the fire. Holes there are where he put his knees as he knelt to hide the cooked meal. Up the top there is a pillar of stone, the backbone of an emu, and the emu's legs are there to see in a shallow cave and on the ground as a line of stone. The lichen on Uluru's southern side is the sign of the smoke from the fire that killed Meta-lungana.

Nearby is a small boulder. That boulder is Meta-lungana. We call this stone 'Meta-bulli'. From it the power of life flows into the land. If you rub the Meta-bulli at the right time, the female lizards become fertile and bear many young. This we know.

We do not know if the Liru (poisonous snake) people killed the sleepy lizard man. But one Kunia man was angry that such a death could occur close to his people. This angry man went to ask the Liru about this thing. It did not go well. When he left, the Liru got angry. The angry young Liru men gathered their weapons and set out for the Kunia camp.

They travelled across the plains from the south-west of Uluru. There despite a warning from one Liru man, the Liru fell upon the unprepared Kunia people. The Kunia were not a fighting people. They were caught unawares. Many were killed. The women wailed in lament. As many as could fled. But they were chased and killed as they ran. The sights of that great slaughter can be seen today.

The desert oaks that stretch between Kata Tjuta (you call that place the Olgas) and Uluru are the young Liru men, who are still advancing. On the ground west of Uluru are two stone areas where the Liru gathered to attack. Gouges on the south west face of The Rock show the passage of the Liru men as they moved upon the Kunia. Plain to see on Uluru's southern side are the marks left by the spears of the Liru as they attacked another Kunia camp.

There is a protection stone where the friendly Liru man called out his warning. Those who rub it can call to the Kunia Dream time people and gain protection during their stay at Uluru. This is true.

The stories continue

From this battle many other stories can be told. The story of Bular, a young Kunia woman who had just given birth is one. Here is another. At Mutitjilda Gorge, a big fight took place. Many Kunia were slaughtered. During this fight, Kulikudjeri, a Liru leader, came upon a young Kunia man. They engaged in single combat. The young Kunia man had great courage, and great skill. With his stone knife he sliced Kulikudjeri's leg so deeply that the point of the knife broke off. Again he attacked leaving a more shallow wound that bled and bled. These two mighty blows remain today as two great clefts in the side of Mutitjilda Gorge.

Kulikudjeri, even as he fell, struck back. He savagely hacked the young man's leg, a wound that killed that fella in the end. The young man crawled away in agony, gouging the watercourse that feeds the waterhole today. Three rockholes mark the place where he died. There his spirit continues to live. Today his blood flows as water to fill the Mutitjilda Gorge.

The young man's mother, Ingridi, saw her son's death. Taking up her digging stick and spitting the white arukwita death spittle on it, she attacked Kulikudjeri where he lay wounded. She struck his nose from his face. Dancing in her grief and distress, she spat death spittle upon him. He died in agony. Then Ingridi painted herself with red ochre and fell to mourning.

Today, Kulikudjeri's nose, a huge block of stone, can be seen on the ground. Above are the remains of his face, eye holes and the place where the nose had been. Streaks on the side of the rock show where his blood flowed. The eastern wall of Mutitjilda Gorge bears the red stains of Ingridi's mourning. Nearby is an open cave, her mouth crying perpetual sorrow. There are white spittle signs to be found around the area. As deadly today as always. So today we do not walk close to the walls of the Gorge for fear of dying. The bodies of the Kunia men lie around. All but one were killed. Some Liru who died lie here also.

Written on The Rock is the story of the end of the Kunia men, which is there forever. From the Dream time to now. And forever.

There is not time to tell you more. Of the Hare Wallaby and Kanjo and the lost boomerang. Of the lizard people who killed Kunia women, or the Mulga seed men, the marsupial moles, the Spirit Dingo or the Willy Wagtail women.

All around us are the true stories of the Dreaming, the Creation time. These are powerful stories. But they are not the secret stories. For the secret stories are stories of life and death. All these stories are true stories. That is the way it is and will be forever.

Nipper looked around. 'I do not talk of the camp of the Women or of Nangaru or Mother place. These are secret places, secret stories. I do not sing the songs or chants that link our spirits to the land and the Dreaming. I only tell you what you can hear. For white fellas don't hear much. That climb up Uluru. You go up there and give no thought. To us that is a sacred way. But we have no voice. Only sorrow. The old ways will be lost if we do not tell the story.

What have you white people got, eh? No respect for the land, no reverence for people. Uluru don't mean anything to you. But for us it is sacred, the place of Dreaming. We carry the Dreaming in our hearts. So I ask you: What is Uluru to you? What meaning does it have?'

Animated conversation broke out and continued for some time. After questions had been exhausted, coffee dispensed, and Nipper thanked for his time, Alan Vizard took him to the door, briefly made contingency plans for the morrow, and returned to his seat. He found a quiet and thoughtful company, waiting for him. 'We have been reflecting on the challenge about our dreaming or lack of it', Colin Freeman explained. 'Whatever else you think about Nipper's world view, it is comprehensive, full and vital. For most of us, I suspect, the religious orientation that we carry is fragmented, disjointed and uncertain.'

❖ ❖ ❖

'Why not?' Helen Wales was the speaker. 'Our world is like that, thirty seconds of commercials and news grab, unconnected, random and mostly transitory. We are children of our time and culture. Orphans in a world cut adrift.'

'The great profanation, a sociologist called it'. Standfast, perched on the edge of his chair, seemed to be addressing a speck on the carpet. 'We live in a time of disenchantment which makes it impossible to share the mythic world consciousness of the people of the Dream Time. How can we go back to that kind of thinking in a technological world? We may hunger for a second naiveté, but we can't have it.'

Jane Orchard grunted. 'Try virtual reality. You can make of the world what you want. Even make yourself up if you want to. Put on a different face every day and try it out. Then take it off at night, like a crumpled dress, and put on a fresh clean one for tomorrow. If you can bear the thought of it', she added.

'This is getting a bit heavy folks', interjected Levi. 'I have been just as affected as you by what Nipper told us. But the key for me is not reacting to his story but his challenge. His story is his story, not ours. We should receive it with respect and learn from it. But we do have to have a story of our own. His challenge, as I heard it, was "What does Uluru mean to you?". He may have meant that literally and if so, I have no clear answer. But if he meant symbolically, something which evokes a religious question in us, then I can buy that. What meaning can it have for us, symbolically, mythically? I would like time to reflect on that.'

Vizard looked at his watch. 'It is almost lunchtime and as far as I can see the weather has not improved.' As if to confirm his statement, a strong gust of wind rattled the windows enthusiastically. 'Let us break for lunch now and reconvene about 2 o'clock. Could I make a suggestion for you to consider over lunch. We are likely to be kept indoors for the rest of the day by the weather. I have long been attracted to Chaucer's *Canterbury Tales*, where, on a pilgrimage to Canterbury Cathedral, the pilgrims told stories to pass the time. My suggestion is that we do the same, taking up Daniel's suggestion that we use Uluru to represent what we want it to represent.

Each of us could then tell any kind of story we wanted to, in any way we preferred. It would break the monotony and Pilgrim Tours would live up to its name splendidly. If that idea commends itself, I would like Daniel to start since it was his idea that we take on Nipper's challenge. What do you think?'

There were signs of uncertainty, nervousness mixed with expectation, and eagerness around the group. Agreement was reached to consider the matter over the lunch break, and to vote on the suggestion afterward. Some other options were briefly canvassed during the meal, including free time and sleeping, but finally the weight of opinion swung back in favour of sharing stories. 'It could be fun', Jane commented, although others had more sober predictions.

When the group met at 2 o'clock, it took only a moment to get agreement on proceeding along the lines suggested by Alan Vizard before lunch. Daniel Levi, a little drawn, made some ritual protests about being first, but everyone recognised that he was prepared to begin. Much settling down on cushions and in comfortable chairs took place. 'No Miller's Tale, Daniel, I hope', commented Freeman. Daniel smiled. 'If only it was that simple', he said. Then he began...

Chapter 3

Daniel Levi

'It may not be known to you that Melbourne has one of the largest if not the largest number of Holocaust survivors in the world outside of Israel.' Daniel glanced earnestly around the group. 'By various means they have found their way to that city. A visible sign of their presence can be found at the Holocaust Museum in the suburb of Elsternwick. There, many Holocaust survivors still able to do so, act as guides, showing the number tattooed on their arm and talking of their experiences. School groups come to the Museum to look at the exhibits, watch films, and listen to their stories. It is a salutary experience to visit that place.

The story of Daniel's grandfather

My grandfather was a Holocaust survivor, although knowing of the anguish and pain, both physical and mental, that he endured all his life, I wonder if survivor is the right word. He was born in Hungary, and just before the Second World War operated a successful business in clocks in an undistinguished city called Nagykanizsi.

Joshua Levi had a passion for clocks, especially antique clocks. He sold and repaired them, and had a well-deserved reputation for his professional work. Always his work was meticulous, his attention to detail scrupulous. Clocks were sent to his small workshop from all over Hungary. My grandfather and grandmother and my father had a happy and contented life.

Then in 1936, or thereabouts, laws were passed by the Hungarian Government restricting Jews from certain activities. Anti-Semitism began to mount. When the war broke out, conditions worsened, and in 1942 police came to my grandfather's shop. They threw the family, who lived above the shop, out into the street, and told them Jews were no longer allowed to operate in that part of the city. My father's family, bewildered by events, moved to a cellar on the outskirts of the city, where in much reduced circumstances, my grandfather tried to continue his business. It was clear what was happening, so arrangements were hastily made and my father was smuggled out of the town one freezing night and sent to relatives in France. Later he crossed the Channel to England.

In 1944, Hungary was occupied by the Germans. Three weeks later, all Jews were herded together and put in ghettoes. A month after that, soldiers arrived with the news that all healthy Jews were to be resettled elsewhere in Hungary to do agricultural work. They were placed in cattle trucks, and arrived at a destination that meant nothing to them, Auschwitz. Four hundred thousand Jews were moved in six weeks. It was on the first day that my grandmother was taken away. My grandfather to his dying day could hardly bear to speak of it. His last glimpse of her was through a body of guards, a terrified twenty-eight year old, who looked fifty, tears streaming down her cheeks. He could do nothing.

At Auschwitz, my grandfather was selected for work. I need not tell you of conditions in the camp. They are well known. My grandfather suffered along with the rest. Few knew of the gas chambers, although rumours were rife. Quotas had to be filled. My grandfather and those in his barracks were chosen. That night, guards entered the barracks and separated my grandfather from the others. He was marched to an office. They checked his name. Joshua Levi, watchmaker, Nagykanizsi.

My grandfather, exhausted and terrified, could barely speak. Already he weighed only sixty kilos. The door of the office burst open and in strode a Nazi Colonel. In his arms he carried a wrapped bundle which he deposited gently on the desk. Slowly he took the cloth off the object, looked at my grandfather and said 'What is this?' My grandfather recognised the clock as a French Religieuse, which had a gilded chapter ring and a black silk background to the dial. It was decorated with ormolu. Its creator was Isaac Thuret, a Parisian. It had been built some time in the 1670s.

Later, my grandfather told me that his response at that moment saved his life. All his love, his passion for clocks came to his lips in one sentence, 'That is magnificent'. When he looked up into the eyes of his captor, he saw reflected there, amusement and respect. In that look was understanding. So my grandfather was set the task of repairing the clock. Who knows how the Colonel knew of his skill. It doesn't matter. Over the weeks of his labours, which restored his spirit and his body a little for he was well fed, he developed a kind of rapport with the Colonel. They shared a love of antique clocks.

My grandfather said of that time: 'I began to believe in God again'. When his task was completed, and as a reward, this being now in the severe winter of 1944, he was sent with the other prisoners to Bergen-Belsen. There, my grandfather told me, 'I did not believe in God any more'. There were corpses piled higher than his head. Human bodies, just skin and bone, naked and abandoned. Staring eyes, open mouths. Perhaps God took a holiday. Perhaps God was ashamed of what men could do in his name. Who can tell?

My grandfather, head shaved, with the yellow star front and back on his uniform of grey, was sent to work in a munitions factory owned by the Krupp family. His particular skill with his hands saved him again. He was involved in constructing timing devices. Two things kept him alive. He knew the war had to end, and there were signs that things were not going well for the Germans; and he hoped beyond hope that one day he might see my father again.

The bombing from the Allies intensified. Several direct hits on the factory killed many workers and injured just as many. My grandfather lost three fingers from his right hand and suffered severe damage to his left knee. He was given adequate medical treatment by frightened guards who had begun to realise that they would need some prisoners to testify for them at the war's end.

My grandfather was still recovering when the town was liberated. On that day, he suffered a complete breakdown of health, as a consequence of which it was a full year before he was well enough to return home. He walked with a pronounced limp. With his fingers gone, he could no longer pursue his career. He told me that he struggled from the station in Nagykanizsi to the outskirts of the city to the cellar which was now the only home he had. It took him five hours. All he had to eat was some sausage and a slice of bread. And when he got there, the building was completely levelled. Nothing was left. Not one brick on another. The cellar had ceased to exist.

Black despair overcame him. His life was nothing. As he stood there, seeing nothing, feeling nothing, a hand plucked his sleeve. 'Joshua', a voice said, and he turned to look into a face he did not recognise. It was a neighbour who had lived some houses away, who had attended the same synagogue many years before. She took him by the arm and gently led him home, talking all the time as if my grandfather would disappear into a black hole of silence forever if she did not.

It was through this neighbour that contact was made several months later with my father who, after the war, had immigrated to Australia. In 1948, they were reunited in Melbourne. My grandfather never worked full-time again. Nor did he speak to my father of the war years. But in the last two years of his life, when he was helping out at the Museum, he seemed to waken again and as if making up for lost time, he took to telling me details of his life in the war, which I have briefly shared with you.[8]

His death eight months ago was the catalyst for this journey. One day he said to me, 'How can you believe in God after the holocaust?' 'How can anyone?' But I could not tell my grandfather, who I loved dearly, that I could not live my life by the trajectory of his. I was Australian born. The past seemed far away. It was not real to me. It was another time. Another country. Sometimes I wondered if it was real to my grandfather any more. Yet his urgency remained. 'The Holocaust must not be repeated!'

The Holocaust continues

It was while these questions were stirring in my consciousness that I read several books on the history of white dominance in this country. And what happened to Aboriginal Australians. One affected me deeply. *Killing me softly* I think it was called.[9] I realised that in my time, and in my country, slowly and imperceptibly, a destruction of a people was occurring every bit as destroying as the Holocaust. Perhaps here I could find an answer to my questions. The question about my responsibility. The question about God. For this was the legacy my grandfather had left me. So as one step I enrolled for this tour.

Daniel continued … .

As I listened to Nipper tell of the fight between the Kunia and Liru spirit people, I thought, 'My God, does it mean that from the very beginning of time, we are condemned to bloodshed and slaughter?' Blood runs down the sides of Uluru. When we see photographs of it blood-red, are we seeing the ancestral story writ plain? Does it have to be like this? There is an old Jewish joke of a group sitting around swapping stories of disasters. One of them says, 'Let's stop this tale of misery. Let us talk of joyous things. What news of the war?'

The legend of the just ones

It seems to me, we are outraged by injustice and go on perpetrating it. For injustice is at the root of the Jewish experience from the beginning. There is a legend, it is said, that has its roots in an incident that took place in the city of York on 11 March 1185.[10] William of Nordhouse, an English bishop, preached an anti-semitic sermon. Within minutes, mobs were running in the streets, seizing Jewish people, and killing them. Seeking to escape the mob's fury, a number of families sought sanctuary in an old disused tower at the edge of town. The siege that took place lasted six days. Deliverance was promised if the Jews would recant and become Christians. Each morning a monk with crucifix in hand would approach the tower and make the offer. But from within the tower, there was no response.

On the morning of the seventh day, Rabbi Yom Tov Levy gathered the families together. 'God gave us life', he told them, 'let us return it to him by our own hands'. All of them, men, women, children, received his blessing. Then they died by the knife until only the Rabbi was left alone. An eye-witness at the time, a Benedictine, Dom Bracton, reported the event this way. 'And then rose a great sound of lamentation which was heard from here to the Saint James quarter ...'

As far as I remember it, Dom Bracton concluded his commentary in the following manner: 'Twenty-six Jews were counted on the watch-tower, not to mention the females or the herd of children. Two years later, thirteen of the latter who had been buried, were discovered in the cellar, but almost all of these were of suckling age. The Rabbi's hand was still on the dagger in his throat. No weapon but his was found in the tower. His body was thrown up on a great fire, and unfortunately, his ashes were cast to the winds. So that we breathe it; and so that, by the agency of mean spirits, some poisonous humours will fall upon us, which will confound us entirely'.[11]

This story in itself is not remarkable in the history of Jewish people. But it had a strange sequel. There is an ancient tradition which goes back some say to the time of the prophet Isaiah, others say before, that claims the world rests upon thirty-six Just Men. Why thirty-six, why men, I don't know. The Just Men are no different from other people outwardly. But they are the ones who take on the sufferings of humankind, so that we do not drown in suffering and despair. Perhaps it is a narrative form of the scapegoat idea. All of the griefs (if not the sins) are brought to this one person as a lightning rod attracts lightning. The outcome for the Lameal-waf, as they are called, is not fun.

In the seventh century, Andalusian Jews venerated a rock shaped like a tear-drop, which they believed to be the soul, petrified by suffering, of an unknown Lameal-waf. In a way, not unlike the rocks of the dead Kunia scattered around the base of Uluru. This ancient tradition and the death of Rabbi Yom Tov, became associated. It is claimed that his own son escaped the massacre. And as legend would have it, God chose, starting with Solomon Levy, to give to the world in each generation, the grace of one Lameal-waf to absorb its suffering.

Now in the twentieth century, the suffering continues. But not just for Jews. For indigenous people, for ethnic minorities, for social lepers of many kinds. Some of my family would say, 'But, Daniel, the suffering of the Jews is unique. We are a chosen people. Our suffering redeems the world'. So it may. Who can tell? There is a prayer amongst us 'If this is what it means to be chosen, please choose somebody else'.

The search for justice

But suffering is suffering, injustice is injustice. We are moral creatures, God help us, and the suffering of my enemy is no less suffering because he is my enemy. I understood this brotherhood and sisterhood of suffering at the foot of Anzac Hill in Alice Springs, when we saw those drunken Aborigines, brawling and lost. Aborigines lost in their own land! How can this be? I remember a question asked of a tribal man, 'What happens when you are in the desert and get lost?'. The tracker looked bemused. 'I reckon when we get lost, we just go home.' Who is responsible, I ask myself, that the unimaginable can occur, an Aborigine can become lost because there is no home any longer to return to, this in their own country.

I share these reflections with you because I do not accept the inevitability of suffering for individuals, or groups, or of a people, a curse running through history that brings a people to its knees. If there is a God so capricious that such is God's will, then I am confounded by the fact that God's creatures are more compassionate and loving than their creator. You may tell me that it is not for me to make judgments as to what God does or does not decree, but as a matter of plain ordinary common justice, why should some be condemned to unending torment and others to unrelieved blessedness, whether in this world or any other. It not only doesn't make sense, it borders on being obscene.

My work as a graphic designer is a labour of love. In my best moments, all sordid concerns of monetary gain aside, I feel like a creator of new worlds. There is beauty in the total process, of conception, of birth, of growth, of maturity, of completion. At the end I feel fulfilled. I think of the Lord God walking in the garden in the cool of the evening, content with a day's work, and I say 'God, I know how you feel!' Complete. At peace.

Of course, such moments are only temporary. The tear of joy and the tear of sadness are made of the same liquid. The wine drunk can be sweet or bitter and sometimes bitter sweet. This I know. But if we have a vision of justice then even if it is an impossible possibility we must expect it, strive to make it possible, live to bring it to flower.

That is why the old prescriptions, the old prophecies, the old cautionary proverbs and wise words are no help here in this desert, in this new land, in this timeless place. We must discover a new destiny for we are all new Australians. Even Nipper, or at least his children. We must discover it together.

This viewpoint is troubling to me. Because it blunts the edges of my Jewish identity. The moral victory of the Jews was that we survived Hitler. That was his failure. But to do it we had to hold our Jewishness tightly together, as destiny or fate. Can we be so clear when external oppression does not draw chalk circles around us and forbids us on pain of death not to step outside?

My schooling took place at Wesley College, a Uniting Church school in Melbourne. A Christian school. Astonishing! At that school there are many Jewish students. We flourished in a climate of religious tolerance. We were taught, and taught others ourselves, a broader vision of shared human endeavour. Of course, such an environment is too liberal for many Jewish families. And too liberal for many Christian families as well. On each end there is a group pulling us back into a stricter orthodoxy. In the middle, there is a place to stand. Not without risk, of course, but free of the frightening certainties of all fundamentalisms. If only we were less sure about everything.

The story of the dying Rabbi

There is a story told of a much beloved and learned Rabbi who is dying. His students are gathered, a few in the small room around his bed, others outside on the landing and going down the stairs. The brightest student is by the bed and so on down to the least able at the bottom. The brightest student leans over and says to the Rabbi: 'Rabbi, do you have any final words for us?' There is silence for a moment and the Rabbi croaks, 'Life is like a cup of tea'. The remark is passed reverently to the next student and by word of mouth makes its way out of the room, down the stairs and finally reaches the least able student.

What does the Rabbi means by 'Life is like a cup of tea'? whispers the least able student. So his question makes its way up the stairs into the room and is finally whispered into the ear of the brightest student. It is clear that the Rabbi has little time left. He is gasping his last breath. The brightest student leans over and whispers urgently in his ear, 'What do you mean, Teacher, "Life is like a cup of tea"?' The Rabbi's eyes open one last time, he gives a small shrug of his shoulders and mutters 'So, life is not like a cup of tea' and dies.

That story, with the humility before the mystery of life that it suggests, may yet save us from continuing that march of folly which has brought the human species to what looks seriously like a terminus.

The Law

Like Nipper, I belong to a people who live by the Law. There is much we share in common. His law cannot be broken. The law that guides us is divinely given. He comes to Uluru, a mountain in which is embodied the story of the Dreaming. Through ceremonial and ritual, he undertakes a continuing responsibility to the land and his people. The Hebrew Scriptures record how, when the people of Israel reached Sinai, they camped in the wilderness in front of the mountain. Only Moses was allowed up the mountain. For them only a dense cloud could be seen. Thick darkness covered the head of Sinai. This cloud they knew signified the presence of God. That sense of the supernatural was intensified when on the third day, lightning and thunder broke out around the summit.

Scholars disenchant the story when they tell us that cloud, lightning and thunder, are symbols associated with the nature gods of the Caananites, which were used to heighten the sense of the numinous, of God's presence in this story. Their storm god was a warrior god so the themes of battle, of blood and conquest, is present in this story also. Still, cloud and fire are part of the story of the escape from Egypt, when God led the people as a pillar of cloud by day and a pillar of fire by night. The symbols are used to give form to the inexpressible.

In any case, this event was holy. Moses returned to the people bearing with him the Law, which has been holy to us ever since. The requirement to keep these laws on pain of death is still taken seriously. The reason is both religiously and sociologically true. Observance of the Law is the source of our identity. Worship gives us a way of not only praising God, but knowing who we are. To forget is also to die as a people.

It is no different for Nipper. Who he is, is bound up with his daily patterns of behaviour. As is true also for a devout Jew. We share a concern that what is most mystical is also most intensely practical, down to the smallest act of compassion in each day's tasks. If his gods are immanent, deep in the land, then the Hebrew God is transcendent, above all human knowing. The thick blanket of darkness covering the summit of Uluru at this very moment would once have been interpreted as God's awful presence. Even Moses, who alone was called up into the mountain, could not look upon the face of God.

Here is a great reverence for the Mystery we cannot name. We also know that life and death are bound up in our faith. There are limits. Some thresholds cannot be crossed. Whichever way you look at it, there is much that Nipper and I share in common, even down to the rejection and suffering, the sense of being socially insecure, and not truly at home in a world that has no enduring place for us.

The storm over the mountain today has sharpened Nipper's question. What does Uluru represent for me? For my own dreaming? If I were Moses, perhaps I would climb up the mountain and converse directly with God. I would ask God why, in a phrase of Woody Allen's, God is such an under-achiever. Why so powerless and undetectable? I remember a story concerning some people who debated the existence of God.

The story of the invisible gardener

Once upon a time, two explorers came upon a clearing in the jungle. In the clearing were growing many flowers and many weeds. One explorer says, 'Some gardener must tend this plot'. The other disagrees. 'There is no gardener.' So they pitch their tents and set a watch. No gardener is ever seen. 'But perhaps he is an invisible gardener.' So they set up a barbed wire fence. They electrify it. They patrol with bloodhounds ...But no shrieks ever suggest that some intruder has received a shock. No movement of the wire ever betrays an invisible climber. The bloodhounds never give cry.

Yet still the Believer is not convinced. 'But there is a gardener invisible, intangible, insensible to electric shocks, a gardener who has no scent and makes no sound, a gardener who comes secretly to look after the garden which he loves.' At last, the Sceptic despairs, 'But what is left of your original assertion? Just how does what you call an invisible, intangible, eternally elusive gardener differ from an imaginary gardener or even from no gardener at all?'[12]

My debate is not just whether God exists, but if God does exist, whether God is moral and just. Is there in this pilgrimage any chance that at the end of it, I will not find again a warrior god, whose servants have hands dripping with the blood of innocents? A God who treats believers and unbelievers with the same indifference? Who takes a holiday when evil and death stalk the land?

These are not questions I happily contemplate. I wish I could forget my grandfather's story. Guilt is the gift of a life-time. Who can receive it and not lose all joy in life? There has to be a path that takes us beyond guilt into the heart of God, where some answers can be found. To tell you the truth, I am frightened to climb the mountain, symbolically speaking', Daniel added hastily, 'because of what I might find. But who can live frightened and trembling on the plain and call it life?'

Ian Standfast broke the silence that followed Daniel's story. 'You are saying, Daniel, that you are seeking a quite particular Australian way of professing who you are?'

'Yes.'

'Is it possible to carry two flags? A national identity and a Jewish identity?. Just as Nipper is Aboriginal and also Australian. How are these aspects to be held together congruently? For the honouring of one can often mean a neglect or spurning of the other.'

Daniel ran a hand through his thick hair, and shook his head. 'Those questions confront us with a dilemma that our time finds impossible to resolve absolutely. Take the case of a Vietnamese migrant to Australia. He is an Australian citizen, but in his heart Vietnamese. He is also a Buddhist. Australian foreign policy directives towards Vietnam can divide his loyalties. At the same time, his Buddhist beliefs are outraged by the public justification by churches of the government's actions. My only answer is that it comes down in the end to a critical moment, a choice. We may discuss the pros and cons for hours. But in the end, some critical incident will require a response and we will choose. That choice will be determinative of all that follows, for good or ill. It is the narrow pass. It is the moment at the crossroads when a choice has to be made for one path or another. That is the agony of being human.'

Helen Wales spoke softly. 'Daniel, perhaps you have answered your own question. You have a choice to climb the mountain or live on the plains in increasing forgetfulness, with your questions unanswered.'

Colin Freeman interjected. 'But to climb this mountain in the search for God is to violate the sensibilities of another, who is a brother like yourself. Perhaps, after all, Uluru is only the question. Here is no oracle to give you an answer.'

The thoughtful silence that followed suggested that no-one wished to respond further to what had been said. Alan Vizard suggested a break which was readily accepted. 'I have taken the liberty of drawing the next storyteller out of a hat.' Alan looked at Lila Sedura. 'Are you willing to go next, Lila?' 'Indonesian women always do as they are told', said Lila, with an impassive face. And then she added with a smile, 'It is a choice we make'.

Chapter 4

Lila Sedura

Lila Sedura began speaking, her soft voice forcing a silence in the room, if she was to be heard. On the coffee table, a bright red flower floated in a dish. Beside it, a candle flickered, and both rested on a tablecloth of intricate design. 'The beauty of the Balinese mind comes in many forms', thought Vizard, recognising Lila's preparation of the environment for her story.

I wish to begin by thanking you for your acceptance and care of me. I am a visitor to your country. You have treated me as a guest. So now I hope to repay a little of your hospitality by telling you my story.

I was born in Bali, the isle of the gods, and live there not far from Denpasar. My father came from Java, but my mother is Balinese. I grew up in the thought world of Bali, which means a divinised world of spirits and gods. Bali is ninety five per cent Hindu. To the Hindu, there are three levels to reality: the domain of the gods, the middle world inhabited by humans, a world of maya, of illusion, in which the truth is grasped only in a fragmentary way, and the nether world of spirits and demons.

The island of the gods

The topography of my island displays this world view well. Balinese turn their back on the sea, which is the domain of the demons, and look to the mountains from which comes 'the wind of the gods'. At the centre of the island is the sacred place Besakih, the Mother Temple, 'the navel of the world,' situated on the slopes of the sacred mountain Sunung Agung.

Since human beings live between the two great spirit forces, benign and malevolent, our daily responsibility is to balance good and evil in a harmony which keeps life in balance. As a small girl, I learned to make daily offerings, one in thanks to the good spirits, the other in homage to the evil spirits to avert disaster. By so doing, an obligation was placed on the gods and the demonic forces to act in a beneficent manner. We burnt incense, made gifts of rice and flowers, and on ceremonial days, entered the temple for cleansing rituals, to achieve reconciliation, to offer worship and appease the spirits of both worlds that impinged daily on our lives and well being.

The temple is the centre of this belief system. There may be as many as twenty thousand on the island and perhaps thirty thousand household shrines. The temples are found in all villages. The first one is the temple of origin, facing in the direction of the mountains where the gods dwell. The second is in the centre of the village, which directs and protects daily life. The third temple is situated at the other end of the village near the sea. This is the least preferred place for this is the temple of the Dead, the place where the ancestor's graves are located.

The Balinese calendar has 210 days in its year. Ceremonial festivals take place each 210 days, when the gods come out of the mountains to visit us and receive special offerings. If you go to Bali at festival times, you will see black and white chequered cloths draped around the waist of temple images of the gods. Here the search for the eternal balance between good and evil is symbolised. We seek to achieve harmony. Like the Aboriginal people, our dance and ritual events are important in keeping daily life regulated. For us the struggle between good and evil is unending. One is never - how do you say in English - desersively?...'

'Decisively?', offered Alan. Lila nodded, 'decisively defeated. That is the source of our art and daily practice, beauty and harmony. This is an endlessly repeated pattern. Life is a continuous recycling of events in a pattern of timelessness'.

When the Hindus came to Bali in about 700 AD, they re-interpreted the spirit religion of the people. They called the spirit of fire 'Brahma', the spirit of water 'Vishnu', the spirit of air 'Shiva', after their principal gods. Brahma is creator, Vishnu maintainer, Siva destroyer. All of these are but manifestations of Sang Hyang Widi Wasa, the highest essence of divinity.

The story of Rangda, Queen of Witches

The unending struggle of good and evil is portrayed in the Barong dance, which has behind it an interesting story. In the mythology of the Balinese, there is a story of Erlangga, the son of a king called Valayana and a Javanese princess. His mother was very ambitious for Erlangga and very jealous. Erlangga did not fulfil his mother's wishes.

He turned to a mystical religious life, spurning all earthly honours. When his father decided to take another wife, Erlangga's mother, beside herself with fury that Erlangga would not dissuade his father, turned by way of revenge to the practice of black magic. She became known as Rangda, Queen of Witches, the personification of evil intention and dark purposes. In the Barong Dance, attended by hundreds of tourists each year, the evil female figure is Rangda, the Witch Queen. She is thwarted but never finally defeated. The circle goes on.

It was this Dharmic consciousness, this Balinese mind, that I brought with me to Australia. Since it has become our practice here, I tell you a story to illustrate such a Dharmic understanding.[13]

The story of the Eternal Word

Ketut grew up in Desa Sunrise at a time when old things were liked because they were old. It was a time when the new had not been hamburgers instead of rice, or jeans instead of the sarong.

Ketut was seemingly an ordinary child, lost in the routine and greyness of ordinary village life. However, hidden in her was a special spark. For some mysterious reason, she had a notion that the world had been addressed by a Special Word. This included birds, animals and plant life.

The question in her mind was this: Who, beside herself, had heard it? Fortunately, Ketut thought she knew the answer to that question. As an act of defiance, she often went out of the village to a nearby sacred place, near a huge heap of rocks. In the secret of her heart, she called the place 'What is the answer to the Great Question?' There she sat down under a tree.

First, she became aware of the vaporous ether around her. She breathed it in rhythmically, as if her whole body was in tune with the cosmos. After a time, the sun shining on the rocks sent warmth through her whole body, a slow fire that warmed her very soul. Time passed. Ketut's ear heard the sound of a running stream. Rising, she sought the water among the sweet grass, bending to drink from its crystal purity.

While Ketut was performing this natural ritual of air, fire and water, she failed to notice assembling around her a circle of birds, animals and plants. 'Why', she said, 'are you staring at me as if I were a mango or a coconut tree?' They answered in a chorus, 'We are here to share with you a secret. It is the magical word SABDA - the ETERNAL WORD, which is common to animals and humans and is heard silently in plants'.

Ketut leapt up. 'At last', she said, 'I have heard the special word that has been given to the world'. The birds and animals said, 'You have heard it because you have the music and the dance of SABDA in your heart'.

In the sacred bonding of this enclosure, Ketut and the birds, animals and plants, formed a circle, and performed the SABDA DANCE.

The birds sang the lyrics of the SABDA in swells of joy. The animals gave voice to the harmonic sounds of various and diverse creatures. The plants swayed in constant and beautiful rhythm, responsive to the inner music of the place called What is the answer to the Great Question?.

From that day on, Ketut knew two things. First, she knew in her secret heart that the world was sustained by the gift of a Special Word. Now she knew its name SABDA.

The second thing she knew was that life was sacred, even to the humblest creature. She must not neglect to affirm the worth of a flower, or a beetle, or a butterfly, or a snake, or a fish. Life had vibrancy and unity because it had been spoken into being from the House of the Eternal SABDA.

Bali under siege

With such a view of the world, imagine the impact upon me of coming into Western ways of understanding Here the magical rich vegetation of my inner and outer life gave way to desert and dryness. I began to see the eternal struggle in a new way. Two hundred planes fly into Bali each day. They bring 1.5 million international tourists and 500,000 domestic tourists, 2 million people flooding into my island each year and bringing with them the aggressive consumerist mind-set of the tourist.

The holy places become tourist shrines. The sacred dances are performed not for ritual purposes, but for the purpose of making money. The spiritual world of the Balinese is being attacked by the secular world view of the tourist. Those who know these things tell me that the island has perhaps twenty years before its infrastructure and traditional village patterns are destroyed irreparably.

This I know for I have felt the struggle in me between the world of the spirit, of beauty and harmony, and the world of owning and using and consuming. What is at risk is the Balinese soul. Soul stealers are everywhere around us. We are losing our story.

For me, it is a raging battle. I feel the conflict of Balinese and Western culture. I hear the call of the old Hindu gods, and the voice of no-god offering me material riches beyond imagining. Since I have been in Australia, I have been participating in a Christian group for overseas students. I have found myself powerfully attracted to the Christian vision for it offers me some hope as a woman that I can be free.

The changing world

In traditional Bali ways, women are excluded from the village councils. Only men decide on what must be done. In Australia, I have learned of women's struggle, of equal opportunity, of views of liberation that go against the caste assumptions, and that of traditional patterns of male and female. I return to a husband who has not changed. I return to a work position in the tourist industry, an industry that is destroying Bali at the very time it is bringing it much needed economic resources and job opportunities.

The population is now too large - 2.2 million people must be fed and clothed and educated. It is only possible through the money the tourist industry brings. But how fragile it is. My heart weeps. For people will only come to Bali while it is beautiful, and daily it is losing its beauty because it is losing its soul. Harmony is gone. The demons of the air join the demons of the sea to destroy us. We are becoming ugly.

It is difficult to find words to convey to you what it feels like to live between worlds, neither fully in this one or that one, struggling to be free from the bonds of the old and yet trying to hold on to its life-giving resources. Who am I now? Which 'world' is mine? I, who can manipulate computers with skill and understand their complex languages, and who, after work, must return to a village where tradition spells out simple duties, submissiveness and passive acceptance of what has always been true, and deference to the wishes of my husband, who, fortunately, no longer accepts this order himself. 'Well, not entirely', Lila added ruefully.

The story of laughter

I have a sequel to the story of Ketut, that has in it my confusion and my hope. You may detect in the story of Ketut, something of the story of the story teller. It goes like this:

As time went on, people began to defer to Ketut. It became clear to those who knew her that she was the bearer of the power of the SABDA. She was invited to speak to more and more groups, including tourist parties who came to her village. One day, she was invited to a women's conference in the United States. Her words flowed as if from the sacred temple, as the waters of Lake Kintomani flow down the mountains to the sawah and renew the island, and flood the paddy fields and provide rice for all.

Her international reputation grew. She travelled much. She developed a professional speaking style. Then, quite unexpectedly, a terrible thing happened. She spoke and there was no power. However brilliant her words, they were empty of depth and meaning. People began to notice and comment on it.

What had happened to her was that she had become beguiled by the illusion in which every truth is covered. The gifts of the Eternal SABDA became more treasured than the Eternal SABDA itself. It led to a crisis of major proportions. Ketut entered, to her despair, the House of Emptiness.

The next few years were ones of intense suffering. Ketut knew that she had lost the art of listening in the whirl of always speaking. Would she ever hear again the creation-making Word? Heaviness lay on her heart. Desa Sunrise for her had become Desa Darkness. She had to find a new harvest in her life. Not the old rice but the new rice.

In desperation, she went back to the place of her youth, to the hidden place of the asking of the great question. As she sat quietly under the tree, she became aware of the rapture in the air. Looking around, she saw all her old friends, the birds, animals and plants. They gather around her in the old SABDA circle.

'Where have you been?', they said.

'I don't know', she answered.

'That's impossible', they replied.

'It may be to you, but not for me. My ears have become blocked.'

All were silent. Then Ketut continued:

'When you know the Special Word, you are in special danger.'

'Tell us how?', her companions asked.

Ketut drew from her garments a sacred lontar. She read from it in studied rhetorical tones. Then, as of habit, she began to sound forth the text's meaning. The words flowed out like a mighty river, impressive, meaningful, profound. That is until someone, who she did not know, began to laugh. He was joined by another, and another, and another, until the whole assembly was laughing as if the end of the world was never to happen. It was high hilarity.

Ketut stopped her reading. The laughter stopped also. In the silence that followed a magical thing happened. Ketut became whole again. The Eternal Word had come again, this time in the form of laughter. Ketut knew in that moment of joy an astonishing truth. It was the laughter that had healed her.

The sacred mountain

Lila looked around somewhat apologetically. 'I hope you understand my little story. It contains a great hope and something of my gratitude to you. When I came on this journey, I was weighed down by all that I am now sharing with you. For me the visit to Uluru is a visit to the holy mountain of this country. In the rich verdant land of my birth, surrounded by plentiful water and the ever-present rice fields, I knew one kind of reality. I lifted my eyes to the hills, as the Psalm says "to the source of my help". But here in this dead heart, in the desert of Australian culture, little that is spiritual grows and water is scarce.'

Where can I find an answer to my questions? Could I come to this sacred mountain and find an answer to my question? Was this the place of the answer to the question? Was this the navel temple that could send flowing from its mystery that life-giving force that could refill my soul and cover this land with a spirit of creation and renewal.

These are fanciful notions perhaps. The word I seek is one through which I can name myself. A word which will enable me to bring a story to my people that has about it harmony and truth that will survive the destruction of the gods. For a people without a story is a people who have lost their soul. This I have learned as I have, in my imagination, watched the dark clouds gather over Sunung Agung, the sacred mountain.

In 1963, the volcano erupted, sending lava down its sides and destroying several villages on its slopes. 'We have been disobedient', the people said, 'we have incurred the wrath of the gods'. I have heard in the night through the storm another word, as the rain has drummed on the roof and water gushes down the path. What it is I cannot yet say fully, but I share with you another story, the meaning of which I am hoping to understand:

The story of the well of life

In Desa Sunrise, Wayan grew up as an ordinary person of his time and culture. If people ate rice, he ate rice. If people danced, he danced. If people went to the sawah to plant rice, he went too. If people went to the temple celebrations, Wayan went to the temple celebrations. If people died, Wayan went with the community to the rice ornamented funerals, when the soul, refined through fire, was released for its journey into ancestorhood.

Except, in doing all these ordinary things, Wayan felt that his life was missing something - perhaps true meaning. All he was aware of on a daily basis was that there was 'more' to life than he was enjoying at present.

It was profoundly difficult to give this sense of incompleteness a name. One day, however, he found himself standing beside a very ancient well. He looked at it in awe. Originally, it was believed that this water had sprung from the earth as a gift of the ancestors. Countless feet had inscribed this belief on the area around the well. Even the stones around the elevated sides, were worn down smoothly at the edges.

So, Wayan, almost on impulse, mounted the twelve steps that enabled him to look down into the depths of this well. Before he realised what he was doing, he shouted: I WANT SOLITUDE! Then a magical thing happened. Wayan received the GIFT OF SOLITUDE. For several months, Wayan lived in the centring calm of this solitude, despite all the human commotion going on around him. Everybody noticed in him this pronounced change. Sadly, this solitude did not last. It was eaten away, as acid bites into metal, by the ordinary demands of everyday life.

So Wayan again became unhappy in the ordinary way of ordinary people. This was an intolerable situation. Already he had received one gift from the well. Was another to be had? He went back to the well, mounted the twelve steps, peered down into the well and found himself shouting into its depths: I WANT COMMUNITY! Marvellously, he received the GIFT OF COMMUNITY.

What a change this GIFT OF COMMUNITY brought back into his life. People picked it up as if they were TV dishes listening in on the movement of his inner world. They said: 'Wayan always knew his position in the community. Now he is doing everything we expect him to do for the good of the whole desa'. They sighed with happiness.

This state of entering into the House of Community lasted many years. Then, in his mature and later middle life, again he had a recurrence of the old dissatisfaction. The acids of care and stress began to eat away at his sense of wanting to do things for others.

All of a sudden, the memory of the well sprang to his mind. He hurried back. Then almost in spite of himself he shouted down into the well: I WANT ETERNAL LIFE! This time, no answer came back. For all intents and purposes, the well might have been empty. So Wayan started to decline. He stopped giving his wife loving glances. He stopped going into the sawah. He stopped going to community meetings. In all, he seemed to have stopped in himself the flow of the river of life.

Wayan's eldest son became very heavy in spirit to see his father in this sad condition of decline. He consulted the local healer, he consulted friends, he consulted far and wide in an attempt to revive and revitalise his father. But there was no evident improvement in his spirits. Perhaps he was even a little bit worse.

Suddenly, the elder son remembered how fixed in his father's mind and life was the ancient village well. He had often told people that it was to him the source of many blessings, and many understandings of life. So the eldest son made a pilgrimage to the well. Like his father before him, he mounted the twelve steps to the top and to his astonishment found himself shouting: MY FATHER NEEDS HELP! The elder son went home bemused and ate his evening meal. The next day, in Desa sunrise, the son woke up. The first thing he noticed was the upright posture of his beloved father. The sun's rays touched his gaunt body and gave it definition, but it also seemed to give him an inner illumination. That day, Wayan followed age-long custom and went out with the other workers into the sawah.

When Wayan came home after the day's work had been completed, he asked his son: 'Who raised me up?' The son, in reply, stumbled over his words. 'I don't know', he said, 'but I will ask'. 'Yes', his father said, 'you ask'. The eldest son quickly journeyed back to the ancient well.

He positioned himself and looked down into the waters, faintly glimmering in the light. He was taken aback. There, at the bottom of the well, he saw the outline of a face, smiling back at him.

He wished his feet had been birds' wings. He literally flew back to the family compound. 'Father', he shouted, 'Father, I saw the face that raised you from the dead'. He stopped, breathless. Then he added, 'And it smiled'. The father stood up as if he were transfixed. For a while he was utterly lost for words. 'So, after all, there is someone who brings us back from the dead'.

The music of the mountain

It is the search for a real word that has brought me here. Such a word would help me know myself. Then when I look into the clear water of the rice field, I will see a smiling face and around it a beautiful and secure world in which animals, birds and plants are part of a harmonious whole. I think the best English word is vision, a way of seeing the Divine will expressed in harmony and peace. It is a vision for my island, my people and for me.

Since I have come to Australia, a rich and favoured land, I have the feeling that here also there is a search for vision, one united country, one people, one common destiny. Is there some help in this mountain? Can one hear at this place the music of a people who are to come?'

Lila ended her contribution with a graceful movement of her hands and a trusting smile in which the beauty of her inner life was transparently evident. Colin shook his head in a bemused way. 'We cannot agree on a flag, an anthem, or whether we are to be a Republic or remain a "possession of the Crown". Right now who can say whether we will ever dance to the same music.'

Jane Orchard, her eyes on Lila, spoke with conviction. 'Like Indonesia, the future we seek has to break the shackles of old ways for there to be equal opportunity for all people. The old gods of power and dominance will not give up their control easily.' 'Perhaps that is why we should not seek them in the mountains', said Ian, 'for the gap between the life on Olympus and the life on the plain is too great. I hope to share what I mean by that when my turn comes.'

So with much to ponder, the group dispersed, each of them seeking their own space, each of them finding words that could belong to them all. Standfast touched Lila's arm. 'You bring the gentle breeze of the gods, Lila. Thank you.' Her grateful smile was response enough.

Chapter 5

Helen Wales

The company that gathered the next day did so with a unity of intention that each member took for granted. It was not simply a matter of giving every member a chance to make a contribution, but rather a sense of compulsion, of rightness about the task and the process they had set themselves. To their eye, the weather outside was not significantly different from the day before. Weather reports on national radio indicated that the low was slow moving. Little change was expected in the weather pattern in the next twenty-four hours.

There was a sense of anticipation as each member settled down. Finally, after the usual greetings, comments on breakfast and sleeping patterns, all eyes moved to Helen Wales, whose turn had been agreed upon the night before. In the morning light, Helen seemed wan and tired. There was a determined cheerfulness about her which spoke of a choice made about what she would say. Minutes later the group understood fully what their random observations had hinted at but not explained.

Helen Wales tells her story

'Three weeks ago', Helen began, 'when we first met as a company of strangers, I introduced myself by saying, by way of a joke, "Wales are an endangered species". Helen paused for a moment. 'I was speaking the literal truth about myself. Exactly ninety-five days ago, when showering, I detected a sizeable lump under my left arm, that I had never noticed before. I rang my doctor when his surgery opened that morning. He gave me an appointment immediately. He was full of good cheer and assurance. "Probably nothing to worry about Helen.

A cyst most likely. We'll have a look at what's there and in all likelihood have it out under a local anaesthetic".

He sent me off to the Alfred Hospital for a battery of tests. We made an appointment for another meeting a week from that date. It was only five days later that he rang me. 'Helen', he said over the phone. 'You had better come to see me today.'

Immediately I feared the worst as one does. But hoping against hope, I went to his surgery at 3 o'clock that afternoon. By his manner, I knew whatever it was, was serious. How serious I could never have guessed. Carefully he went through what the tests revealed, including naming the cancer I had. On the way home, I went to the local library and looked it up in a medical text in the reference library. Word for word the reference read:

Malignant diseases manifest themselves in a variety of ways.
..... . Thus for example, painless swellings in the breast or in muscle may indicate an underlying carcinoma or sarcoma respectively.[14]
There followed descriptions of various cancers and their effects.

My doctor explained the treatments available, the course he would recommend, the possibilities that were involved. But his heart was not in it. The bottom line was, the cancer was incurable. At worst, I had six months, at best eighteen. The one blessing was that there would be little pain until the very end, when drugs would ease my dying. I remember staring at his tartan tie as he spoke, trying to assimilate the news, trying to come to terms with what was in effect a death sentence. I don't know how I got home that day. I walked into my flat, aware of how empty it was. There was no more lonely person on the planet that day. No one more devastated.

You know already that my husband and I separated about seven years ago. He found he was attracted to other women, younger other women. Reconciliation was never possible. Our two children are grown up.

My son, Andrew, lives in Germany where he works for an import-export firm. Melanie, my daughter, is married to a farmer who works a property on the NSW/Victoria border. They were too far away to call on for support. The numbness was going. The fear was beginning.

During the next week I told nobody. I had the strange irrational feeling that if I spoke of it, my disease would be confirmed. You know, speak of the Devil and he appears. I became totally obsessed with my condition. I couldn't think of anything else. I wept, I raged, I cursed God, then apologised and begged for a miracle. One night, I smashed every plate in the kitchen I could lay my hands on. Another night, unable to sleep, I walked the streets for hours. I lost weight. My work became affected. Friends became worried. I fell into depression and contemplated suicide. How lonely it was. And how self-pitying.

One morning, as I got ready for work, I stopped myself in the bedroom and looked into the mirror. 'If this goes on', I said to the image of myself looking back, 'you will have no life left at all. Pull yourself together!' I sat down on the edge of the bed, rational for the first time in two weeks, and began to explore my options. Taking a pen and paper to the dining room, I began to write out what possible courses of action were open to me.

It was clear that I needed time to think. I rang my father, who no longer comes to the office, although he still owns the business, and told him I wanted three months long-service leave. He was immediately alarmed. 'I couldn't be spared just now - was I ill? - I wasn't due for long-service - he had not been well lately.' I expected him to tell me it would damage the economy, increase unemployment, and bring the government to its knees before he was through!

But I insisted. 'Why now, Helen?' So off the top of my head I said, 'Because I have won a trip to inland Australia and I have to take it now or lose it'. Helen turned to Alan: 'So that's how you got me. I couldn't tell my father the truth. It was a coward's way out'.

The dream of the dark tower

That night I had a dream. I was riding a horse at breakneck speed across a prairie. Behind me there was the sound of baying dogs. Looking down, I realised I was the horse, and looking closer, that my legs were covered with scales. Ahead of me, the ground rose to a fairyland castle, the kind used to illustrate children's fairy stories. I knew I had to gain the castle before the dogs caught me. But as I approached, the moat began to shrivel up, light fell away from the gold and blue walls, doors and windows disappeared. In the place of the castle was a black tower whose top went up out of sight. Frantically, I scrambled around the base looking for a way in.

The sound of the pack became louder. They were very close now. Then on the side of the black tower, I saw wooden steps nailed like a ladder. In an instant, transformed again into myself, I sprang on to the first step and began frantically to climb. But as I did so, the tower melted away. I was left climbing the steps without anything to hold on to but the step above, which seemed somehow to be self-supporting. With each step, the scales on my body began to fall off. As they did, they fell singing into the void. I thought I recognised the song. With each step, I felt lighter, unencumbered.

It was then my terror began. For as I put my foot on the next step it cracked under me, forcing me immediately to grab for the one above, which also gave way. I struggled hopelessly as each step broke under my weight. The void opened beneath me. Just as my strength was giving out, the last step appeared. Above it was the cloud which had shrouded the uppermost point of the black tower. Without any choice, I sprang from the last step, even as it disintegrated, into the thick darkness of the cloud. And I fell into nothingness, accelerating down to earth. I woke up vainly trying to fly, flapping my arms like an idiot.

Around the room, there was the sound of people letting their breath go. Helen looked up at the sound, but did not stop. 'It was only after I woke that I recognised that the scales falling off had been singing a hymn I remembered from my childhood:

How vain the worldlings pomp and show
The night approaches now ...'

But each scale was singing different variations. Some I recalled:

The night approaches now, the day has passed forever
The night approaches now, there is no other
The night approaches now, kept fast the lights' memory

Others I forget. You may think it strange, when I tell you the dream was not a frightening one. When I woke, despite its heavy air of menace, I felt renewed somehow as if I had escaped from a prison.

It was a few days later, reading in a somewhat desultory fashion, that I came upon two pieces of writing by chance. Leafing through a copy of *Markings*, [15] I came across what looked like a line of poetry recorded on New Year's Eve in 1951. The line read: 'Night is drawing nigh'. Dag Hammerskjold had added '...and if this day should be your last ...'

I turned to New Year's Eve in 1952. There it was again: 'Night is drawing nigh', with the addition, ' How long the road is'.

But the entry for New Year's Eve 1953, took my breath away:

'Night is drawing nigh -
For all that has been - Thanks!
To all that shall be - Yes.'

My eyes filled with tears. I couldn't read the print. I cried for twenty minutes, tears of joy and release. Don't ask me how this came about. Perhaps sub-consciously I had recorded those words when I read Hammerskjold's journal years before. I can't tell you. But when I needed them, these words were there. They were given to me. I cannot say more than that.

The story of the Samurai and the Tea Master

The meaning of my dream was further illumined when I encountered the second piece of writing. It was an ancient story from Japan about a Samurai and a tea master.

Once, as the story goes, a tea master accompanied a great Samurai warrior on a journey to visit a distant city, where the Samurai was held in high esteem. It was known throughout the region that the Samurai was a warrior with courage and skill. In addition, he was honoured for his wisdom and understanding.

So impressed was the tea master that when the Samurai was sleeping, the tea master would slip into the Samurai's armour and walking through the city received the honour and respect of its citizens, who took him to be the Samurai. The tea master more and more grew under the adulation. It was possible for him to imagine that he truly was a Samurai.

But in the area, another Samurai lived, who was cruel and brutal. Hearing that another Samurai had arrived in the city, he sought him out. Not realising that it was only the tea master in disguise, the local Samurai challenged him to a contest of skill.

The tea master was terrified. He was no warrior. He knew what a cruel and dangerous fighter the Samurai was. His folly had condemned him to death.

Filled with shame and fear, the tea master returned home, took off the Samurai armour, woke the sleeping Samurai and confessed his stupidity. He humbly asked for forgiveness, for taking the armour and dishonouring the Samurai's reputation. The wise Samurai forgave him, but told him that the tea master must meet the Samurai's challenge. He would die whether it was because of his folly of pretending to be a Samurai, or because he was a swordsman of no great skill.

The wise Samurai then told the tea master to prepare a proper tea ceremony while he thought out how he would deal with the rival Samurai on the morrow. A proper tea ceremony is, of course, a great art. It requires careful preparation, formidable discipline, and studied attention to exact detail. The tea master, who was an expert in his art, was quickly calmed by the performance, which so moved the wise Samurai that he suggested a way of meeting the cruel Samurai the next day. He should meet the Samurai not as another warrior, but as a master of the tea ceremony.

The next day, the two met for the challenge. The cruel Samurai dressed in his finest battle armour was truly frightening. The tea master, for his part, wore his own ceremonial robe while carrying the wise Samurai's armour under his arm. Upon arriving at the challenge site, the tea master put the armour aside. Then with the practised art of his craft, he began the delicate preparations for a proper tea ceremony for the two of them.

The cruel Samurai began to laugh. But as he watched the extraordinary skill, concentration and discipline of the master of the tea ceremony, he fell silent. Soon the cruel Samurai began to wonder and grow afraid. 'If he prepares a simple tea ceremony with such skill and precision', he thought, 'he must be a great swordsman indeed'.

The cruel Samurai, overcome with fear, prostrated himself on the ground, removed his sword, offered it to the tea master, and begged forgiveness and mercy for his arrogance. This the tea master granted. The cruel Samurai quietly left the city, and the tea master then turned with gratitude to the wise Samurai for teaching him the secret of self-acceptance - to be who you are. [16]

This story further illumined my dream for me. I knew that I could never overcome the disease that threatened me. As long as I fought it on its own terms, resisting, avoiding, denying the true reality, I was without real power and would certainly lose. Even the respect of my friends, which I attracted by pretending to a courage and stoicism I did not feel, was part of the charade. I knew that when the challenge had to be met, I had no defences.

As I reflected on the story further, it seemed to me that a source of wisdom in me, the wise Samurai, was suggesting that to wrap myself in armour was no answer. I had to let myself be without pretence. I could hear the scales falling into the void singing 'the night approaches now'. If I must face my adversary without weapons, then what was left me? Only a despairing leap into the dark cloud. That is where my dream had left me.

But the story suggested another way. In the story, the tea master conquered by being himself. He had returned to authenticity and become what he was, a tea master. I knew how difficult it is to come to self-acceptance. Who was I really?

Memory is hope

These last weeks, before we left on this trip, in order to answer that question, I have been revisiting the places where I grew up. I drove back to the town where I was born and visited the house my parents had owned when I was a child. Then the school, and the swimming pool, and a cafe in the main street. It has a different name now and has been extended, but it still smelled of fish and chips, just as I remembered.

I went through the phone book and found there the name of one of my old teachers who had retired in the town. Now in her eighties, I hesitated to call. Would she remember me? But I did call, and received an invitation to afternoon tea. We talked for a long time. She seemed as sharp as ever. As we were standing at the front gate, as I was taking my leave, she said a wonderful thing: 'Thank you, Helen, you always brought the sun with you'. She kissed me on the cheek. I, who was moving into night was the bearer of the light! What a delicious paradox. But the comment gave me hope and strength.

I read somewhere once that memory is hope. That return to my childhood, to the days of my youth, to the church where I was married, and the hospital where the children were born, and the journey through those quick bright years of my life, brought me calm.

I had begun, in my own way, to prepare the tea ceremony in the presence of my adversary. I laid out with precision and great discipline all that I had done. The task has brought more light than I believed possible. And my adversary became threatening no longer. The words of Dag Hammerskjold became my words: 'For all that has been - Thanks! To all that shall be - Yes'. With Hammerskjold, I knew what it was to be free, to be able to stand up and leave everything behind without looking back. To say yes. To be able to say yes!.[17]

The story of death in the market place

I had ceased to run away. You will know the story that is told in many ways about the time in the market at Bagdad when Death jostled a servant of a rich man. The servant distressed, ran home, told his master what had happened, and immediately took horse for Samakand, another city some distance away. Later in the day, the rich man met Death in the marketplace and chided him for upsetting his servant. 'I did not mean to upset him', Death replied. 'It was only a reflex of surprise at finding him here, since I have an appointment with him tonight in Samakand.' How futile running away is.

So, I have sought to make my peace, to enter into that self-acceptance which trusts the purpose that can be found in all otherwise meaningless events, if one searches for it. Yet I was troubled by one other element of my dream. At the top of the ladder there was only cloud. When I leapt into the cloud, there was nothing.

When I booked my passage on this journey, it was because of the lie I had told my father. I wasn't sure I wanted to go. The brochure looked attractive. The wonderful photograph of the Rock attracted me. Yet I worried about whether this was the best way to spend four precious weeks.

My thoughts on the tour have been increasingly turning to that image of the Rock. At times it seemed to take on aspects of the dark tower. Then at Alice Springs, while looking at postcards, I came across the photograph in which the Rock was completely black, standing out above the plain, like my dark tower. And I was racing across the plain again pursued by the hounds of hell, or whatever they were. You remember how we looked for glimpses of Uluru as we drew near, only to see it briefly, through mist and dark cloud. Then it disappeared completely and we have seen nothing of it since.

It was yesterday as I listened to the conversation about how the symbol of the cloud has been used in many cultures to speak of the presence of God, that I understood. We will all one day take our final step and direct ourselves to that cloud into which we will fall. From this side of death we cannot expect to know what that leap will mean. But on the way, we have caught glimpses of that which is splendidly real beyond all imagining.

We have each been seeking to answer the question of why we came on this journey and what we came into the desert to see. I am not sure that I chose to come on this journey, although in a strange kind of way I did. Looking back on it now, it seems as if I have followed a course mapped out for me. As if my dream contained within it a hidden imperative to go to the mountain.

The story of time and the Grand Canyon

Thinking further on our conversations together, it has come to me that what I was seeking was acceptance of my own life and all that it has been, salt and pepper, good and bad. That certainly is true. I have imbibed the desert air, and it has been wonderful. But there was more here. A memory stirred in me. I recalled an incident that occurred many, many years ago, when two friends and I took a tour of the USA. The tour included a trip to the Grand Canyon. We arrived at lunchtime, had a quick meal and then went sightseeing along the rim.

The next morning, I woke up early, and, being unable to sleep, I dressed and went out of the hotel. The sun was just freshly awake also. I walked for about twenty minutes and then, defying all the warnings not to do so, I stepped off the path, scrambled through some bushes and stood right on the edge of the Canyon. I was completely alone. I knew, as I looked down to the bottom of the Canyon, I was looking at all geologically recorded time. The tour guide had spoken of it as we had walked the day before. All of recorded time! I stood there in the silence, looking at this wondrous sight with the question on my lips: 'What does it mean?' The multi-coloured void gave no answer. The silence continued.

Then to my ear came the distant sounds of someone running. The sounds grew nearer, louder. Suddenly, quite suddenly and unexpectedly, the bushes burst aside and there was a young boy, hair awry, breathing heavily, his breath hanging in the air, his aspect wild. He stopped up short at the sight of me. He looked into my eyes. Then, without a word, he turned, plunged back through the bushes, and disappeared. I heard the sound of his running feet diminishing into the distance. In a moment, all was as it was. The silence was complete. I stood alone with my question.

Honestly, for a time I thought I had imagined this strange, unreal appearance. It seemed surreal. Reason told me I had not. Yet there was no evidence that it had happened at all except that I had been given unexpectedly an answer to my question. The meaning I sought was not in the geological stratas I contemplated, but in the human figure who asks questions of the void. The enduring metaphor is the human. We are significance-seeking creatures. So in that engagement between that which is there, and we who reflect on what is there, an explanation arises that gives us meaning. Perhaps God is the source of the idea of God, I thought.

Remembering that incident again gave me an answer to the question I had raised for myself. I have come here to stand again at the intersection between time and eternity. This Rock began to form sixty million years ago. It has been here in its present form perhaps thirty million years. I have a life that has reached its use-by date of fifty-four years. I say that without self-pity now. Against sixty million years, what is fifty-four? Against the countless aeons of God's eternity, what is my life but a blink of an eye.

Yet the immensely comforting thing is that we do not travel this journey without grace. There is food and drink on the way, manna in the desert, an inn after the long day's journey, a place at last to rest. In my early days of knowing about my illness, I was angry for long periods of time. No-one had taught me how to confront my own death. Everyone was bound up in a conspiracy of denial. People hurried through murmuring sympathy and turned with indecent haste to discussing fashion, or football, or the latest Royal scandal. I might as well have lived on the moon. Isolated, frightened, without resources. No mother craft to whisk me away. Only my own footprints on a lunar landscape barren of all spiritual sustenance.

I don't feel like that now. I learned that others had crossed the Frontier before me. The true wilderness to be understood and crossed was within. So I have laid out my tea ceremony with dignity, integrity and love. I seek only now to sip the tea with joy, perhaps a little ecstasy, and a full heart. I can wait now for the gentle coming of understanding, which is the 'night that now falls'.

Helen finished her story with a slow gesture of her hand. Vizard thought that for an instant, it was a blessing, but her hand fell gently to her lap into the silence of the room. Colin Freeman was the first to respond. 'Helen, thank you. I have been deeply affected by your story. It took courage to tell us, to be so personal and honest.' Helen Wales stirred herself. 'I have never been a political person. I have done no great deeds. I have been a competent mother, a disappointed spouse, a moderately successful business person. But all these have been roles I took on.

Of course, I have done charitable things, given to famine relief, worn a red nose, visited the sick and attended Mass on high festival occasions. These are things I have done. But who I was, I never really knew until I had to deal with this final stage of my journey. I can't say I have any vision of what this nation might become. What future should be lived into. How we should negotiate the shoals and reefs of this last decade of the twentieth century. All I know is that what is most deeply personal is most general. We all share this common destination, however differently we describe it. I have come to value all of you in this room very much. In our short time together, in our small ark, we have sailed wondrous seas. Colin, let our gratitude be mutual. For me, what I have is enough.'

As Vizard left the room for the agreed break, he paused at the door and looked back. Helen Wales stood with her arms around Jane Orchard. The young woman was sobbing. Others sat quietly or moved around searching out coffee cups. Lila was smoothing out the cloth under a vase of flowers, her features covered by her dark hair. As Vizard stepped outside, a handful of rain splattered on the concrete path. He moved off into the storm, leaving the calm centre behind.

Chapter 6

Colin Freeman

Colin Freeman clapped his hands. 'I need your attention. When science speaks all must be in attendance and filled with reverence.' It was clear that Freeman intended to enjoy himself as he began to take his turn in sharing the reasons for his presence on the tour. After Helen's first session of the day, the lighter atmosphere created by the genial scientist was welcomed.

I was destined for a scientific career from the first day I walked into a class of 'Singles' Doubleday, teacher extraordinaire, avowed Marxist, dedicated atheist and a lover of all things scientific. Not for him the middle way. Life was passionate, a crusade of truth against error, a drama in which rationality set out daily to rout the superstitious and credulous. Among the latter, he numbered Christians, politicians, poets, artists, all musicians and Americans, who were the running dogs of capitalism, a well-known scientific phrase. His irreverence was refreshing. His ironic barbs deliciously acid.

To a twelve year old he was irresistible. I was totally captivated. Within two weeks, I was a true believer. Science alone was my destiny. All doubt was cast aside as we tittered, lunged, stumbled and puzzled our way through the mysteries that lay before us in test-tubes, equations, mechanical experiments and theoretical explorations. The magic of mathematics broke open before me as we applied numbers to the daily events that cried out for interpretation and explanation.

The story of the Chieftain with three sons

I remember well one story of a Chieftain who had three sons and seventeen camels. When he died, he left instructions that his oldest son was to get half of the camels, his second eldest a third and the youngest a ninth. No matter how you tried to divide the camels up, you ended up with a fraction or a part of a camel, which, of course, is no camel at all. The elders did not know how to fulfil the wishes of the Chieftain.

One day a wise man rode by on his camel. He listened to the dilemma confronting the elders. Then he took his camel and tied it up with the other seventeen, making eighteen. He gave half, which was nine camels, to the eldest son. He gave six camels, which was a third to the next son. Finally, he gave a ninth of the camels, which was two, to the youngest son. That left one camel over, the wise man's own camel, which he promptly mounted and rode away.'

Freeman roared with laughter. 'Irresistible, isn't it! Irresistible!'

'Singles' took his lead from Jacob Segal, the biologist. 'All that happens in the world is nothing but matter and its motion'. The world, 'Singles' preached, could be understood adequately only by the scientific method. Matter was not only the natural cause of our sensations, but also the prime cause of all processes of nature.

Only that exists which is observed and observable. I wrote in my notebook with reverence his four foundational propositions:
1. The world is knowable.
2. The world is by nature material.
3. Being, nature and matter are primary.
4. The world is self-sufficient.

They were heady days. The days of certainty and delight. We knew who we were, and who were the enemies of progress. It was the age of innocence. The inner logic of our life was clear. If it was possible, it was necessary. And science could make it so.

I need not spell out for you the slow wakening to greater awareness and doubt that followed. My days at university were filled with confusion and self-recrimination. I began the first year with the well-established scientific assumption that I was a detached observer setting siege to an inert universe of matter, whose secrets I would probe and remorselessly uncover, by the exercise of reason and its greatest tool and accomplishment, inductive processes and the methodology of scientific investigation. The words we used were control, experimentation, measurement, behaviour, and above all predictability.

Quantum physics and the upheaval of worlds

Then QF struck. That is to say, Quantum Physics, which turned my mechanistic predictable world upside down. As Alexander Pope wrote:

Nature and Nature's laws lay hid in night,
God said: 'Let Newton be', and all was light.
It did not last, the Devil howling 'Ho!
Let Einstein be', restored the status quo.

At the risk of boring you, I'll sketch out some of the more intriguing aspects of the third wave of scientific explanation of the world. You may have seen a homeless person approach a rubbish bin to search for food. If unobserved, this is what will happen. But if the person concerned looks up and sees you watching, he will walk past or stoop to tie up a shoelace, or look up at a tree with great interest, and so on. Being observed changes what is otherwise a predictable course of behaviour.

A quantum particle, say an electron, does not have a precise location and motion at one and the same time. That is, position and momentum cannot be studied simultaneously The more precisely one quantity is measured, the less precise the other quantity becomes. An electron can sometimes behave like a wave and sometimes like a particle. You can construct an experiment to display its particle-like properties, and another to display the wave-like properties, but never both together. Wave and particle behaviour are therefore complementary aspects of a single reality, as the scientist, Nils Bohr, argued. Which you get, wave or particle and what it reveals, depends on how you choose to engage it.[18]

But the mystery deepens. Experimentation, it revealed, led to the 'collapse' of the wave function. So long as a quantum system is not observed, the wave function evolves predictably. It obeys, what is called Schrodinger's equation.

But when the system is inspected by an external observer, the wave function suddenly behaves erratically, without predictable patterns, in violation of Schrodinger's equation. So like our derelict who behaves in two completely different ways, one when nobody is looking and one when he is being observed, so at the sub-atomic level the same phenomenon has been demonstrated.

There is a conclusion to be drawn here, which destroyed the very foundations of my prevailing scientific world-view. Observing a quantum system interferes with its behaviour. In other words, none of us is able to be a detached observer. We change reality by our interaction with it. We can only know some things by looking for them. But looking for them not only makes them visible, it makes other aspects of the sub-atomic realm invisible.[19]

There was in all of this a paradox that was bound up in what has been called the dilemma of Schrodinger's cat. Forgive me if my enthusiasm is overwhelming a common courtesy to make sense. But it will help me explain myself to you more fully.

The paradox of Schrodinger's cat

Schrodinger proposed a hypothetical situation. A cat is placed in a box with a flask of cyanide 995. The box also contains a radioactive source, and a geiger counter that can trigger a hammer to smash the flask if a nucleus decays. The whole system is, you see, inter-related. After a short period of time, the process is in a state where a probability of one half suggests a decay has occurred, and one half that it has not. If the entire contents of the box and contents, including the cat, are treated as a quantum system, we are forced to conclude that the cat also is in a situation of two states: dead and alive.

In other words, the cat is, in this theoretically possible situation, both dead and alive, which is impossible in the usual restraints of reality, but not in the other reality quantum physics projects. As another scientist called Wigner pointed out, when discussing these matters, the mind of the experimenter (or the cat) causes the wave function to collapse. However you read it, Wigner claimed, consciousness was a significant participant in the whole process, unavoidably and unalterably.

Something had happened to my world. The foundations had crumbled, its certainties were swept away. When I looked for predictability, I found only a sea of uncertainty. The classical picture of reality that 'Singles' Doubleday had given me was gone, destroyed forever. Questions I had suppressed emerged. A proton, I knew, weighs 1,834 times as much as an electron. Why 1,834? There was no answer. It just was. My scientific world view, which described reality one way, could help us significantly. True. But it was only one possible explanation, only a description. These descriptions did not constitute the total reality we sought to embrace.

Even more bewildering, we constituted the reality we saw by the way we engaged it. We were really away with the fairies here, and the nymphs and shepherds and all. The universe at macro and micro levels bound together in a dazzle of infinity. I couldn't accept it because I didn't want to open myself to what 'Singles' by fiat had dismissed, the category of mystery. You could believe anything. We could not capture this mystifying universe in our language because we had nothing to compare it with.

Why not accept myth as a surer guide? The Greeks, in one account of creation, had Earth, Erobus and Eros as the first beings. Eros issued from the egg of Night which floated on Chaos. By his arrows and torch, he pieced and vivified all things, producing life and joy. Weird you say. No weirder than the stories physicists were telling each other about the stuff of reality.

The story of the bees

It was while I was in this state of confusion that one day I visited a friend of mine in the country who keeps bees. Fascinating creatures bees. With an interactive social system so completely at one with itself that it leaves you boggle-eyed at its symmetry. I was helping him sort through some magazines he had collected on bees over the years and I came across a story in one of the magazines, some competition or other. It wasn't even a good story, but I read it, and as they say in the classics, everything fell into place. The story went like this :

Once there was a man who kept a hive of bees at the bottom of his suburban garden. The bees, as bees do, set off each day seeking nectar in the gardens of surrounding houses. The neighbour, who lived next door, hated bees and if the truth be told, was frightened of them. Rather than complain, he set out to get rid of the bees. At a suitable time, when there was no-one at home, he turned on his hose and tried to frighten the bees by hosing them. The result was a painful bee sting, and no change to the operation of the hive.

On another occasion, again when the house next door was vacant, he sprayed pesticide over the fence. This time some of the bees died, but within a few days the bees seemed to recover and appeared as busy and numerous as ever. At the next opportunity, when he thought the house was empty next door, he lit a large fire near the back fence, spread damp leaves over the blaze and watched with satisfaction as the wind carried the smoke over the fence into the vicinity of the hive.

It was then than things went horribly wrong. Suddenly, the owner of the bees, who had returned undetected, burst out of the back door. To his eye, his bee hive seemed to be in flames. Leaping down the steps he ran towards the smoke. His neighbour watching him, saw him suddenly clutch his heart, falter and then slowly sink to the ground in severe pain.

Some days later in hospital, recovering from his mild heart attack, he was visited by a remorseful neighbour, who confessed that he had lit the fire deliberately, and also that he had tried unsuccessfully on other occasions to kill the bees. It was due, he confessed, to his fear of bees. The sick man looked at his neighbour for a long time. He knew he was a good man and that his actions were the result of fear not either malice or spite. 'I have a task for you', he said. 'I want you to move my hive from its place against your fence to the front garden'. Then he gave instructions on how this was to be done.

Some days later, wrapped in safety clothing, his neighbour approached the hive cautiously. His mouth was dry, his hands trembling. He knew that he must carefully lift the queen bee from her fortified position at the centre of the hive and move her to the new location. Only then would the other bees follow. What agonies he went through. Would the bees swarm and attack him? Would he damage the queen? It was a long time before he had identified the queen and lifted her up, and by then the bees were all over him. He could feel the vibration of their humming all around him. They crawled over his arms, his back, his neck, and his head. But they did not attack.

He was conscious suddenly that the resonance of their humming was sounding within him, moving along his arms and legs, entering the inside of his skull, penetrating to his heart and stomach. The humming went into the deepest recesses of his being and he became completely possessed with bee-song, as if the song of the hive and his life's song were one. His identity and their identity seemed fused in a seamless harmony of sharing. He stood possessed as he had never been before in his whole life. He had become one with the intricate complex of the hives sociality. For a moment all boundaries dissolved. Oneness was all.

The next day he returned to visit his sick neighbour, who, when he entered the room, knew immediately that a profound change had occurred. The visitor gripped his neighbour's hand. 'I have brought you some honey', he said, 'from our hive'.

After reading that story, I was able to name what had happened slowly and inevitably to me. I had been overwhelmed by wonder. That which I had merely observed and sought to manipulate, had become alive in me in a startling way. That which I had regarded as dead matter was alive energy. I had been overcome, taken captive, by the interactive nature of all that I encountered through my experiments.

I was not just an observer, but a participant, actively engaged in a mysteriously open universe that sends out radiant explosions of active energy, constantly alive, constantly evolving and changing. There was a harmony and balance to it that was so arresting that it was like a song. Here I was, the most practical and prosaic of creatures, confounded by wonder that was the antithesis of all I had believed and lived. I now know that all conversions which seem to happen in a moment are only the culmination of a long process of minute deflections, subtle changes, enlarging questions, a slowly rising crescendo that reaches a moment of insight when all that has been is overthrown in an instant.

I began to see the scientific quest in a new way. No less scientific, but now open to mystery, to the unexpected, sensitive to the provisional rather than committed to the dogmatic. I believe that once when someone told Mark Twain that such and such was the will of God, Twain responded 'Who found that out?' So for me now. I had been led into a new place where questions were more important than answers. The human participant is a primary factor. I now inhabited a living universe in which the pattern and order of events could not be denied. Paradoxically, even as the religious question opened up for me, I became a better scientist, one no longer locked into dogmatic reductionisms, but free to learn more truth. For much more was now permitted.

The story of the flying machine

It has raised for me sharp questions about science and its role. I can illustrate that best by repeating a story by Ray Bradbury called *The Flying Machine*:[20]

In the year AD 400, the Emperor Yuan held his throne by the Great Wall of China. He was sipping tea when a servant broke into his reverie proclaiming that a miracle had occurred. 'Excellency', the servant declared, 'a man is flying'. After further explanation, the Emperor decided to see for himself. Following his servant, the Emperor looked up. Sure enough, a man was flying. To the eye, he looked like a new dragon in a land of ancient dragons.

Seeing them, the man called down, 'I fly, I fly'. The servant waved back. The Emperor Yuan did not move. Instead he looked at the Great Wall of China, stretching into the distance, that had protected China for countless years from enemy hordes, and preserved peace for years without number. He saw the town peacefully sleeping, beginning to waken to the morning sun and the Emperor became thoughtful. 'Has anyone else seem this flying man?', the Emperor asked. 'I am the only one, Excellency', the servant said. 'Call him down to me', said the Emperor, which the servant did. Looking around, the Emperor noticed a farmer, early in the fields, watching these strange events.

'What have you done?', asked the Emperor of the flying man.

'I have flown in the sky', replied the man.

The Emperor repeated his question.

'I have told you', said the flier.

'You have told me nothing at all', said the Emperor touching the apparatus, covered with coloured paper, that had enabled the man to fly. The Emperor, by questioning the man, learned that this flying machine was the only one in the world and that no-one else knew of its existence, not even the man's wife, who thought he was making a kite.

The Emperor invited the flier back to the Great House. Once there, he summoned his guards to capture the man and he called for the executioner. 'What have I done?', asked the flier and he began to weep. 'This man asks', said the Emperor, 'what have I done? He does not know himself. It is only necessary that he create without knowing why he has done so, or what this thing will do'.

The Emperor turned to a nearby table upon which sat a machine that he himself had created. Taking a small golden key from around his neck, the Emperor wound up the delicate machine and set it going. Birds sang in tiny metal trees, wolves walked through miniature forests, tiny people ran in and out of sun and shadow, fanning themselves with miniature fans, listening all the time to the tiny emerald birds and standing by impossibly small but tinkling fountains.

'Is it not beautiful?' said the Emperor. 'Here I have made birds sing. I have made forests murmur. I have set people walking, enjoying leaves and shadows and song. That is what I have done.'

'But so have I', pleaded the flier. 'I have found beauty. I have smelled the sea and seen it beyond the hills, looked down on woods and towns. I have soared like a bird, felt the wind, smelled the sky in the morning. How free one feels! How beautiful it is!'

'Yes', said the Emperor sadly. 'I know it must be true. I wondered what it must be like. But I am also fearful for the man who is to come.'

'What man?'

'The man who does what you do and builds a flying machine of bright papers and bamboo as you did. This man has an evil face, for such a man, flying high above, might drop huge stones upon the Great Wall of China.' No-one moved or said a word. The Emperor nodded, the axe flashed, and the inventor died.

'Burn the kite and the inventor's body and bury the ashes together', said the Emperor. Then to his servant he said, 'Hold your tongue and tell the farmer in the field to hold his. Regard it as a dream or a vision, that of a man flying. If ever the word passes around, you and the farmer will die within the hour'.

The Emperor watched the guards digging a pit for the ashes. 'What is the life of one man against those of a million others? I must take solace from that thought.' He took the golden key and wound up the miniature garden again. All was set in motion. Tiny people walked in forests as before, and among the tiny trees, flew little birds of high song and bright blue and yellow colour, flying, flying, flying in that small sky.

'Oh', said the Emperor, closing his eyes, 'Look at the birds, look at the birds.'

The dilemma of the scientist

'I tell this story,' said Freeman, stretching his arms high, 'because it poses for me the contemporary dilemma of the scientist. Am I an emperor, who properly fears the outcome of unreflective development? Am I an explorer, who pushes beyond human limits and threatens the social order? Who is right? Is beauty to be set against beauty? Expediency against progress? Protection of what we have, against freedoms we cannot control?'

I am working at the moment on ozone depletion. Currently in our society, short-term goals are pursued in order to secure economic solvency that threaten long-term viability of many plant and animal species. I have enough contact with bureaucrats in a working week to know that there are many petty emperors in parliamentary seats, who have no desire to glance at the sky and see the threat that looms above us. Or the will to take courageous decisions.

So in a time of enchantment from the rebirth of wonder in my soul, I am daily disenchanted by the mundane processes that shape and direct our corporate existence. I spend my time in a tiny miniature garden, wound up by processes that predetermine tiny people to do predictable things, in prescribed ways, in established patterns.

I booked for this tour because I needed to fly again, to inhabit vast places, to smell the earth and the wind and the sky. And to again inhale the heady air of mystery, to feel again that slow breaking out of wonder before the very singularity that Uluru is.

It has become for me a symbol of all that I yearn for in this infinitely mysterious universe. I read claims made to solve the riddle of the universe. I am troubled now by the arrogance that is implicit in such claims. Stephen Hawking, one of the great mathematical minds of our time, anticipates a complete theory, the 'theory of everything', which would lead to the ultimate triumph of human reason and a knowledge of the mind of God.[21]

But what will we know if we have such a comprehensive theoretical explanation of the universe? Only a theory. It will inevitably prove in time to be inadequate. New mysteries will burst upon us. Our language will fail as it inevitably must before that which defies description. The universe will go on eluding us, and inviting us to participate in its fulfilment.

Science has been for me a journey out of comfortable certainties to a stance of contemplation and meditation before the mystery of creation, of which Uluru stands, however we seek to explain it, as a singular example, pointing us through its very singularity to contemplate our own uniqueness and the call to participate in the honouring and treasuring of this world. This is a world in which we have been set free to create.

Do not ask me to be specific. Hear my story as the confession of a conventional man, who one day opened the door of his small house, and slipped into a world of beauty, magic and splendiferous possibility, beyond all expectation. What that means, I am still in the process of discovering. Learning to fly has its own strict requirements.

Archie shook his head. 'I don't know how much I understood of that, Colin, but it sounded impressive. Not exactly your usual speech at the smoke night for the footy club. But I get your drift. You haven't any more clue as to where you are than the rest of us.'

The group burst into spontaneous laughter. 'I know where I am', interjected Daniel, 'within arm's reach of lunch'. A chorus of approval broke out. Moments later, after the usual appreciation for what had been shared, the group fell to eating and drinking together.

Chapter 7

Jane Orchard

'I would like to begin with a story', said Jane Orchard. A distant roll of thunder could be heard as she began speaking. 'It is appropriate that the noises far off are dramatic. My story comes from the realm of fantasy, "the faculty of strange and whimsical imagining". So make yourself comfortable; it may take some time.'

The story of the daughter of regals

This is a story about Chrysalis, daughter of the Phoenix Regal, who is approaching her 21st birthday. On her 21st birthday, Chrysalis must demonstrate that within her is the magic that will enable her to rule over three kingdoms.

The rulers of the three kingdoms are her implacable enemies. One of them is Count Thornden, huge, bitter and as shaggy as a wolf, with a wolf's manners and appetites. Another is King Thone, rotund, urbane and malicious. The third ruler is Queen Damia, beautiful, devious and cunning.

The three kingdoms of Lodan, Canna, and Nabal were interdependent, for Canna had no wood, Lodan had no metals and Nabal had no food. Each ruler, therefore, desired the throne, and plotted with their own mage to overturn Chrysalis and her mage Ryzel, formerly Regent of the throne. In their turn, each cannot trust the other.

They gather together with representatives of the kingdom to see if Chrysalis can pass the test of true magic and become a Regal. A Regal was both human and creature, fully human and fully real, and possessor of the true magic. Regals had ruled the three kingdoms before her. Each had a gift which was symbolised in their Regal name: Cockatrice, Basilisk, Gorgon, the Phoenix, Wyvern and Banshee.

True magic could not be touched unless you yourself had magic. No test of the many undertaken had detected any magic in Chrysalis. Yet she was determined at midnight, when she turned twenty-one, to touch the stone upon which her father, the Phoenix Regal, as all other Regals before him, had sat. If she had no magic, her death was certain. She had learned that she had no power over fire, or wood, or stone.

Even the wooden sceptre, which her father had given to her mage Ryzel, was slippery to her grasp. It evaded her clutch. She could not seize it. Each ruler came in turn that day to gain control. Thone used blackmail, threatening the destruction of the kingdom through the power of his mage who controlled fire. Then Thornden, who with the assistance of Ryzel finds Chrysalis unprotected, seeks to rape the princess and by violence to control and overthrow her. If necessary his mage will use the power of the wind to force compliance. Finally, Queen Damia demonstrates her power when her mage conjures up the form of a dragon, who threatens to destroy all in the palace.

This last threat is the greatest threat, because it is believed that all dragons have been slain, the last by the Basilisk Regal, a crime beyond measure. To conjure up a dragon meant that against all knowledge there remained one in existence, hidden somewhere in human form. In addition, Damia has formed alliance with a rebel leader Kodar, whose men had infiltrated the palace. All is at risk.

Each approach by one of the three rulers in turn is resisted, overcome, and conquered by Chrysalis' resolute will. Her enemies do not turn her. It is only her own doubt, her own despair that can do that. She faces her test alone. The three rulers seek her death. Her mage has deserted her and sought alliances to save the kingdom from bloodshed. All she has to rely on is a promise from her father that she will come to splendour as he did.

The time has come. She approaches the throne to touch the stone, alone, without hope. As she reaches out, suddenly, her enemies act. A fierce wind is set at her by one mage, while another conjures up the dragon whose fierce fire threatens her destruction. Her own mage, responsive to her command, does not intrude. As the wind presses her back from the magic stone, and the fire of the dragon creeps nearer, Chrysalis cries out for the wooden sceptre her father had given Ryzel her mage. Ryzel throws it to her. She struggles to hold it even as it conspires to slip from her hands. With one arm around the staff and the other cupping its end, she edges forward.

All is brought to a moment. In her memory is her past failure when she touched the stone, a failure known only to her. But this time, she touches the stone with the wood. At that moment the blood which the Basilisk Regal had shed comes to life in her. All weakness was swept away in wild glory. A roar burst forth - a challenge against every foe and traitor in the realm. The dragon line restored again to the kingdom burst forth in her. She becomes a Real, a true daughter of Regals. For the blood of the last dragon had sunk deep into the flesh of the Regals. Her father had procured the limb of the Ash so that the ancient magic might aid the birth of something new in his daughter. That was why her father called her Chrysalis. A new order, a new world was to break forth in her, the true daughter of Regals. Stone and wood combined to call her to her destiny. The realm was hers.[22]

When I first read that story by Stephen Donaldson, I was unexpectedly moved. It was a time of choices for me: to become engaged to Damien; to seek employment; to imagine a destiny where I could find personal, familial and societal satisfaction. As I reflected on the story, its parallel to my life became clearer.

The name Chrysalis was one. What was I to become? What kind of creature was I? My confusion was not uncommon. To be a young woman in today's society is a nightmare. Voices whispering 'be this', 'be that'. Should I seek a career or be a married woman destined to write on census forms 'home duties'? Should I travel? Do further studies? Be celibate, be politically correct or counter-culture?

Should I become a female 'power dresser', or a this goes with that creature, or Nike shod in preference to stiletto heels and Opium perfume? Choices of how to be female or feminine are a reach away in any newsagent. Perhaps some tattoos with a life ahead spread over a Suzuki motorbike. Jane screwed up her face in mock horror. 'The possibilities are endless.'

In the story, they crystallised into three big temptations. To assail the throne by treachery, by brute force, by sexual manipulation and cunning. It became clear to me that my generation had to make choices which were never presented to my mother or other generations of women.

The slipperiness of the sceptre was dead right. We could not take up a future defined by male precedent or paternalistic traditions. Whatever the patterns of the past, we had to craft our own future with reference to a new order, a new creation. We could not afford to put our trust in accepted alliances for we would be betrayed. We had to make our own decisions alone and unaided.

It sounds overly dramatic to talk like this, but how can I or any of my friends discover our own pattern of being fully human, fully real, that is our victory, our creation, our authentic selfness? You will appreciate how each of us wants to be a daughter of Regals, with autonomy and choice. Romantic visions, however, encounter the reality of what is possible and unavoidable also. I didn't want to fall in love, at least not yet. I am not even sure I want to be married. The burden of responsibility is very hard to carry.

The dream of fading away

In the end it was a dream I had that forced me to confront all these questions. The time of this dream's appearing is significant. It was a day in which light rain was falling, a grey heavy day, common enough in Melbourne, which depresses the spirit.

I was in my flat alone, feeling isolated and cut off from everyone. At about four o'clock in the afternoon, as I sat in my armchair looking out over the wet and dripping garden, I fell into a light sleep, vaguely depressed, vaguely discontented and totally disconnected from everyone. Who knows how long it was before I began to gain a sensation of travelling. It was the sense of moving that began my dream. Oddly I seemed to be the actor in the dream, yet watching myself at the same time, an observer taking notes on what was happening.

In the dream I was returning to the farm where I grew up as a small child. I was coming home to tell my family of my wedding. The air was filled with farm smells; the sun shone. When I arrived, my family and friends all seemed to be in the house staring out of windows or standing expectantly on the front porch. I was feted and approved. Then before I could blink, I was being fitted in my wedding dress, adjustments being made, merry chatter, pins in mouths, cups of tea and singing of old hymns and modern ballads. I remember 'Climb every mountain'. Another scene began.

Next I was in the house alone, answering the telephone, hearing my mother say, 'We will only be delayed a day or so, the creek's impassable. It has been raining for hours'. Slowly walking through the house, emptying teapots, throwing out dead flowers, listening for the scuttling of mice, worrying about whether there was enough wood chopped, I began to shimmer a little, to get blurred at the edges, to feel faint.

Every time I passed the mirror I looked at myself. I seemed to get thinner, less substantial. I became terrified. I was wasting away, becoming less and less real, more and more insubstantial. I went to brush back my hair. My hand passed right through as if the bones, muscles and veins had no weight, were bloodless, were ghostly.

Panicked, I ran into the bedroom and put on my wedding dress. Parading back and forth before the mirror, I began slowly to gain solidity. Colour seemed to flood back into my dream. A voice over the radio said 'It's the real thing'. I returned to my old self. But only as long as I kept wearing my wedding dress; when I took it off, I began to fade. So I kept it on, humming to myself, listening to the radio, waiting for the return of my family and friends.

When they returned, I rushed out to meet them, wearing my wedding dress. They sprang out of the cars and began to applaud. I curtsied but couldn't straighten up again. Bent over, I noticed for the first time that underneath my wedding dress, I was wearing hiker's boots. At that point, my observer self wrote 'Loss of true home' on her notepad. Abruptly, I woke up, conscious that whatever was going on in the dream had to be understood. 'Loss of true home' drummed in my head.

To climb a mountain

That is why Helen's dream moved me so much. It had the same feel to it, as if my deeper self was bringing to my attention issues I refused to address. As a researcher, I am often in libraries so I took the chance to read some books on the interpretation of dreams. The conclusion I reached was that the best interpreter of my dream was myself. It was while stacking up some books on the library that my eyes fell upon a picture of Uluru. The song in my dream came back to me 'Climb every mountain'.

Damien was due to go off on a field trip for two months. Why should I not do the same, I thought? So I booked for the tour, hoping for time to think through the images which constantly process before my eyes. I was driven by the need to answer for myself: what does 'loss of home' mean?

These last weeks I have come slowly to the conclusion that for me, it meant 'loss of self'. I have been living in my mother's house, my mother's dream for me. It was warm and comfortable. I was approved and applauded. But it came clearly to me that if I went unthinkingly forward, I would become crippled, never able to stand up straight again. Was I who was called to be a daughter of Regals, I told myself, falling for one of the temptations, to forge an alliance which would give me power and safety at the same time? If such was the case, I would never grow, never be 'fully human, fully real'. So the dilemma presented itself. What should I say yes to? What no? And what would guide my choice?'

Jane moved uncomfortably in her chair. It was only by revisiting these two stories that a deeper explanation emerged. If I took the fantasy as a dream and the dream as a story, new insight emerged. The fantasy as dream reminded me of two things. The Regals always married commoners, for their destiny was the love of the people. Their 'regal' nature ensured peace for all, but was hidden in the every day pattern of being ordinary. I did not have to be extraordinary to be real, only myself. The dream as story now said to me that the isolation which leads to fraying can be overcome by a total commitment to a wider community, a broader vision, which saw beyond home and farm (my mother's world) to include in itself a sense of the 'kingdom', which to me spelled 'people'.

As I listened to Nipper talk of Uluru, I felt ashamed I had resolved to break my dream by climbing the mountain when we arrived here. I learned from him that to do so would hurt Aboriginal sensitivities. Why then the refrain' Climb every mountain'? I saw that here too in the *Sound of Music*, Maria was breaking out of a closed destiny to find a new world. The mountain to be climbed, therefore, involved a journey. It was to seek a higher standpoint, a change of perspective, a more comprehensive view of what my generation of women can offer to an emerging Australia.

To come to Uluru was to be confronted again by a mirror of myself. It has thrown back a choice. To join the ants scurrying over the face of the holy mountain, oblivious to what is being done by that action, or to face the task of climbing within; I must scale the heights of self-doubt and listen to the promise that there is a new birth taking place in my generation which will have significance for all that is to come in the 21st century. My people are the present generation of young women. If we can dare to risk, all will be saved.

The story of one stick, two stick

I recall an African story which is called 'one stick, two stick'. Knowing that his end is near, an old man gathers his family, friends and other villagers around him. To each person, the old man gave a stick with instructions to break it. With some effort, each managed to break their stick in half. The old man comments: 'A soul without anyone can easily be broken'.

Then the old man gives another stick to each person. This time he asks for the sticks to be gathered into bundles of two or three. 'Now break these sticks', he commands. No-one can break the sticks when they are gathered together. 'We are strong', the old man says, 'when we stand together. Together we cannot be broken'.[23]

Our shared life together these last weeks, the story of the cultural bonds of tribal people, an enlarged sense of what a new woman can hope for, has lifted me out of the narrowness of vision I left home with, nursing with it sentiments and judgments that in this desert place seem trivial and inconsequential.

So I answer the question, 'What do you come to Uluru for?' this way. All of us have an image of Uluru in us. It is a call to a more inclusive vision than we have yet entertained in Australia. The Rock has reflected back to me light I have been earnestly seeking, about where to go next. I have not found demons on the mountain. I brought them with me. They have fallen silent before the vistas opened up by our being here together. This tour has given me an enduring image of what centredness can mean.

I read somewhere once that the root meaning of 'diabolical' is to pull apart, to fragment and to scatter. The symbolic, by contrast, unifies and brings focus. I have had that chance here with you and I thank you for your love and care. Jane placed her hand over Helen's for a moment. I have written a story of my own out of the courage and hope you have given me. And I have taken the liberty of setting it in the same world where a princess discovers she is a daughter of Regals - truly human, truly real.

The story of the princess and her gift

It was the custom in the kingdom, its place and time I do not know, that when a princess became a certain age, a special ceremony was held. During the celebration, the princess was taken to a chair alongside the throne. In a liturgy as ancient as stone, at the chosen moment, the princess rose, affirmed her loyalty to the throne, the people and the land, and then declared the gift she brought to the realm. It was this gift which she would use for the good of the people. So it had been since time began.

Ursula, daughter of the present king, had arrived at the age of presentation. Tomorrow evening she was to mount the steps to her chair, declare her allegiance and announce her gift. But Ursula knew on the eve of the ceremony that she could not name her gift. She had nothing to offer which compared in any significant way to the gifts of her predecessors.

At 3 o'clock in the morning, not being able to sleep, she had come to the portrait gallery in despair. There was in her, for all her accomplishments, no vision of what was uniquely her offering. Nothing certain, nothing special, no inner conviction, nothing.

Cold and desperate, she sat in the women's section of the Family Hall. Around her were fifteen portraits of those who had preceded her. Each known for her gift, remembered, for good or ill, for their contribution to the people of their time.

She looked at the proud face of Martha, who had announced her gift as the gift of right order. She had become expert in the law, and a wise counsellor remembered for charity and justice. Beside her hung the portrait of Anna, mother of three sons, who had declared her gift to be that of nurture. She had cared for all, not the least her own family. Her sons had lived straight and true, shaped by her oversight and unfailing love.

Clara was less revered. The gift she had offered was celebration. During her time there had been many festivals, but little celebration, for she had proved superficial, vain and self-serving. The fierce countenance of the future warrior queen, Annabelle, looked down at her. Mother to her people in a time of threat and conquest, she had led the armies of the realm against its enemies. Three times she had saved the land, and died at last, as she had promised on the day of her presentation, with a sword in her hand, defending the honour of the people.

Her eye moved from portrait to portrait, remembering the story of women frozen there, recalling their gift offered, their lives lived, their destiny now complete, the fulfilment of the promise declared on the day of presentation.

Ursula sat there in the cold hall, the torches throwing light only on the faces of the dead. Her own darkness deepened. Her doubt and despair grew. Who was she to be? What did she have to offer? It was as she bowed her head that the whispering began. First one voice, then another. These crowded out by others seeking to be heard, urging that her gift be Ursula's gift. Take the gift of wise administration. The gift of a warrior. The gift of nurturing care. Become a patron of the arts, a gatherer of knowledge, a lover of life, a voice for reasonableness.

The room became filled with the sound of their voices. Voices urging, 'be like this', 'become like me', 'do it this way'. Hands over her ears, Ursula fled from the hall, down the steps, past sleeping guards and vigilant guardian lions, on to the vast grassy common beyond the huge brass doors of the keep.

Tired at last from running, Ursula stopped, exhausted and spent. She stood swaying, alone in the damp air, her head filled with a cacophony of insistent voices, demanding, pushing, urging. Slowly she lifted her head to gaze at the huge mountain that rose behind the palace. The light of the moon fell upon its rocks and crags, spreading illumination and darkness together.

As she looked, the light of the moon seemed to fall with purpose upon her face and shoulders so that she was bathed in a gentle, soft luminosity. The voices stopped clamouring, began to fade, and soon were not heard at all. The silence in her grew. It became a large silence, filled only with light. She gazed at the mountain for a long time. As she waited, the world sang with silent harmony. Joy began to fill her soul. Ursula began to dance.

When the sun began its first moves to morning ascendancy, she returned to the palace. At the bronze gates, the guardian lions made no movement as she mounted the steps. As she entered, a silence crept through the corridors of the palace, a calm peace, a restful quiet. To speak balm to the voices within. To bring silence to the crowded hearts of men and women that joy may grow, perhaps this was the greatest gift of all, the silence of true Presence.

Holding her gift deep within her heart, Ursula, daughter of the king, stepped confidently towards her destiny. Behind her, brilliant with snow, the mountain sparkled in the sun, blood-red as dawn broke upon the world again.'

After Jane had finished her story, there was much stretching, but no-one spoke. Something of Jane's gift worked its magic in the hearts of the listeners. Outside, no sound was heard, as if the elements of the earth, wind, rain, lightning and thunder, had stopped to listen also. The faculty of strange and whimsical imaginings had cast its spell.

Chapter 8

Ian Standfast

Ian Standfast's comforting presence gave the company reassurance as they turned expectantly towards him. There was a quietness of spirit about Standfast that spoke of deep resolution of significant conflicts. Around the room there was speculation about the trials and tribulations that had brought the elderly cleric to this time and place.

The third journey

I have been ordained a member of the Church for over forty years, but am now retired. I was married for forty-two years, but am now widowed. I have been father to two children and head of a family. I am now alone. I begin, therefore, a third journey symbolised by this tour.

Once, when I was young, I set off on a quest for meaning and intimacy. When I met Janet and we married, my second journey began with the guiding, sustaining presence of another. Together we built a world that had two foci: family and ministry. That second journey lasted for over forty years.

Three years ago, one day, without warning, Janet was stricken with a virus. I remember its sudden attack late one afternoon. She had difficulty breathing. Speech was laboured and difficult. We called an ambulance and within minutes she was receiving oxygen. She died at ten o'clock the next morning, without speaking, only the message of her eyes which said to me 'Ian, my love, I know this is goodbye. Understand always I did not want it to end this way'. We held hands, our suffering mutual, words beyond us, just the grip of our hands and the uniting of our hearts to sustain us.

Standfast faltered for a moment, but quickly recovered. 'I knew fear at its deepest then, a terror of abandonment by God. And the devastating loss of Janet was a grief too intense to be borne. I, who had ministered to countless others in their time of bereavement, was now bereft of all comfort, all words, all consolation. In this nameless fear, I encountered the boundaries of language. I, who had been a wordsmith all my working life, was now without words.'

Fear can rob you of speech for different reasons. Sometimes what we have to deal with fills us with such uncertainty and disquiet that our response is too weak for words. We are forced to silence. Sometimes when a sense of violation or anger, of pollution and defilement sweeps over us, then words are inadequate to describe the outrage we feel.

There have been other times when I have been overcome with awe. Words here are unnecessary or superfluous. But here was a speechlessness out of abandonment. I was powerless. I was immobile, diminished, without words or gestures. Despair began to knock at the door. The fear of nothingness began to fill me. That, I learned, is the fear that kills. It leads to the death of the self. Standfast paused. 'But I get ahead of my story.

After Janet's death, I continued working in the parish for two years, but my heart was not in it. I retired last year, when I turned sixty-five. It was not that I had lost faith, you understand, only that I had lost the thread that connected me to all that had meaning and significance. I came to terms with my loss, as we all must, after a fashion. And I began to ask myself 'What does God require of me?' Since my youth, I had lived for no other purpose than to be God's servant - a somewhat quaint idea to the present generation I found in my religious education classes at the High School.

But what now could I do? It was in this period of living in the desert of the soul that I came across the question of Jesus to those who had sought out John the Baptist. 'What did you go into the desert to see?' Quixotically, it suggested a course of action. I too should go into the desert, literally as well as spiritually, there to find some answer. The stipend had never been fulsome though adequate. So I sought a desert experience within my financial means. Pilgrim Tours seemed just right. To come to this mountain with my questions seemed right. I bought a ticket and began, what I called, my third journey.

The story of Esau and Jacob

I would like to share with you a familiar story. [24] Isaac, the son of Abraham, married Rebekah, the daughter of Bethuel, the Armenean. In time, she gave birth to twin boys. The first born, Esau, was covered at birth with red hair. The second was born clutching his brother's heel, and so their destiny was bound up together. He was called Jacob. Esau, the hunter, was the favourite of his father, but Rebekah loved Jacob most.

One day, when Esau came in hungry from the fields, Jacob offered him some stew in return for the birthright which was Esau's because he was first born. Thoughtlessly, Esau agreed. Even now the old phrase 'a mess of potage' is used of those who despise long term opportunities for a quick advantage. After eating and drinking, Esau went his way, but that one act of renunciation became the hinge upon which the future destiny of the brothers hung.

So it came to pass that when Isaac was dying, he called Esau to him. Isaac asked Esau to kill some game, prepare a special meal and then Isaac promised to bless Esau before he died. Rebekah was listening. Hoping to secure the blessing for Jacob, she ran and told him what was planned. She urged Jacob to prepare the meal before Esau returned and, since Isaac's eyes were dim, he could substitute himself for Esau and thus receive the blessing. Jacob protested. Esau was a hairy man, Jacob of smooth skin. 'If my father touches me', said Jacob, 'he will detect who I am and I will be cursed, not blessed'.

Rebekah, however, acquired some skins which she used to cover Jacob's hands, dressed him in his finest clothes and sent him into his father with the food. Isaac surprised at the quickness of Esau's returning, and hearing Jacob's voice, not Esau's, stretched out his hand and stroked the hairy goat's skin which covered Jacob's arms. Reassured it was Esau, Isaac gave his blessing to Jacob. So Jacob, by deceit, acquired the blessing, servants, flocks, grain and wine, and became Lord over Esau. The inheritance had passed to Jacob.

The story of Jacob's ladder

When Esau returned, it was too late. His father blessed him with a prophesy and died. Esau's hatred against his brother swelled up and he plotted to kill him. Again, Rebekah stepped in and warned Jacob of Esau's intentions. So Jacob fled and on his journey came to a place where, using a stone for a pillar, he sought rest for the night. It is this incident that is my concern.

For here, Jacob dreamed of a ladder whose base was on the earth but whose top reached into heaven. The angels of God were ascending and descending on it, thus signifying commerce between earth and heaven. There Jacob received a promise from God, and with that promise the assurance that God would not leave Jacob until all that was promised would come to pass.

Jacob woke up, terrified out of his wits. The source of his fear was that God was in this place and he knew it not. He called the place Bethel - house of God - and using the stone on which he had slept as a base, built a pillar, there to commemorate this realisation that here was God's place.

There is in all mythologies a story or stories about commerce between heaven and earth. Some of them are still alive, presupposing a cosmology of a three tiered universe, heaven above, earth in the middle, hell below, much as Lila indicated is still common in Bali. In Aboriginal legends, a story is told of a Casuarina tree that reached into the sky. This tree was the link between the sky spirits and those of the earth, but it was cut down in one story or destroyed by lightning in another. Human destiny as a consequence is to be sought in this world and no other.

The tower of Babel is another story about aspiring to heaven, and building the means to get there. Dante pictured purgatory as a seven-levelled mountain that the soul must ascend.[25] At the top was the Garden of Eden from which humankind had been cast because of the disobedience of Adam and Eve. We, on ascending the mountain, would return to what we have lost. Mt Sinai, as Daniel reminded us, was a place of Divine-human encounter.

But these last years, I have not found such symbolism helpful. The image of God it contains has for me now no efficacy.

The story of where God will be found

Let me explain by reference to a story. As the story goes, a devout person came out into the desert and knocked at last on the doors of Mystery. 'What do you want?', came a voice from within. 'I have preached your word to others, but they had no willingness to hear. So I have come here to talk with you directly myself.' 'Go back', came the response from within. 'Here there is no word for you. I have sunk my hearing in the deafness of mortals.'

Janet's death made me realise that it is in the depths of the human that I encounter God. Not in some place of mystical vibrancy, but in the suffering and struggle of being openly, vulnerably human. I sat by her bedside as she gasped for breath, and every breath was charged with the mystery of existence. For if this breath was not followed by another, life would become death. A whole world, infinitely precious to me, would disappear with that last gasp. Some words of Kazantzakis came to me in short bursts and flashes. Later I looked them up:

> What is this life, what secret yearning governs it?
> There was a time I called its lavish longing God
> and talked and laughed and wept and battled by his side,
> and thought that he, too, laughed and wept and strove beside me.
> But now I suddenly feel I've talked to my own shadow!
> God is a labyrinthine quest deep in our hearts;

Weak slaves, think he's the isle of freedom and moor close.
All the incompetent cross their oars, then cross their hands,
laugh wearily and say 'The Quest does not exist'.
But I know better in my heart, and rig my sails;
God is wide waterways that branch throughout the human
heart.[26]

While I sat with Janet, I began to question much that I had so
glibly preached. I remember visiting a colleague some weeks before
he died of cancer. He looked at me. 'Ian', he said, 'I am now having to
live what I preached'. In my turn, the images of God, supernatural,
majestic, eternal, unapproachable fell away. All I could speak of God
came down to this one small human hand clutched in mine.

How far from true comfort the folk wisdom:

God unterrifying
Death unworrying
the good accessible
the bad endurable.

I was Jesus in the garden of Gesthemane before a silent
impenetrable Other, praying into a night from which all hope and
light was gone. I was Jesus on the cross, abandoned. I was Jesus without
hope of resurrection, for my life was gone in another's, and there was
no tomorrow. That is why Uluru is a comfort to me. It does not point
us to the sky. The eye travels over its blunt surface and returns to the
earth again.

70,000 fathoms

For me, the Christ event stands out on the plain of human history as
this giant Rock rears above the flat surface of the desert, stretching
for kilometre upon kilometre as it does. The Rock is that upon which
my whole life's enterprise rests. And I am learning that it returns me
again to the metaphor of the human, to this mysterious pathos-filled
existence in which love seeks to stay alive out of the very soil of all
that negates it. The word for it is incarnation.

The Christian vision speaks of a God become human, whose
presence among us provokes us into activities that are risky, painful
and costly. Absurd if you did not believe that the purpose of all this
bewildering complex of creation is on our side. I think it was the
Danish philosopher, Kierkegaard, who said 'faith is swimming in water
70,000 fathoms deep'... He did not offer any comment on drowning
in 70,000 fathoms deep. It came down to this in the end I realised. 'If
the universe is alive, is the purpose for which all life flows benign
or not?'

For all of its terror, the image of 70,000 fathoms is a comfort. To reduce life to a thin layer of soil over rock, to have no depth, however terrifying, out of which to live, would be absurdity beyond bearing. Here in the desert, I have learned that there is life beneath the sand dunes. There are deep reservoirs of water that if we could but tap them, we could make the desert bloom.

It is as if we have here not just a personal metaphor, but a corporate and national image as well. Here at the heart of our continent are resources which, if brought up from the depths of our collective existence, could transform and renew our land. Is it outrageous to suggest that it is the Aboriginal people, keepers of the spring for countless generations, who can act as midwives to that new birth?

Everywhere there is a loss of value. The loss of a reverence for places and people. A steady decline in the strength of public commitment to shared possibilities. There is a decay of idealism, a moral cynicism, a world weariness in which all value is melted down into the base metal of profit and political advantage. We have become, to our bewilderment, made in the image of market research. Today's values are, amoeba-like, spawned out of the ironic contempt for yesterday's standards. We are slowly imploding into a black hole of utilitarianism, where there is no ground upon which to stand.

'I fear', said Ian, apologetically, 'I am beginning to sound like an old man too fond of preaching for anyone's good. including my own. Let me return again to the story of Jacob for the sequel to his story has bearing on what I want to say'.

The story of the return of Jacob

The time came for Jacob, as it comes for all of us, to come to terms with what he has been. He makes the decision to return from exile and seek reconciliation with Esau. In preparation for this homecoming, Jacob sends Esau a message to say that he is returning and asks forgiveness. When his messengers return, they tell Jacob that Esau is coming to meet him with four hundred men. To Jacob that sounds suspiciously like a military force. He divides his company into two camps, reasoning that if Esau attacks, he will at least be able to save half of his possessions and people.

Jacob is filled with anxiety. He instructs his servants to gather two hundred female goats and twenty male goats, two hundred ewes and twenty rams, thirty milch camels and their colts, forty cows and ten bulls, twenty female donkeys and ten male donkeys. Separating the droves, Jacob tells his servants to give them as gifts to Esau with space between each offering, so that each present is followed by another and another. That night Jacob took his two wives, two maids and eleven children across a ford of the Jabbok and returned alone to the camp, there to prepare himself for the confrontation with Esau that is to occur on the morrow.

That night, alone, with his conscience and memories, the record says 'he wrestled with a man until daybreak'. What man? Himself or at least the self he might have been? Or the man in him who would run away again from the reality awaiting him across the river, Jabbok, which is possibly a play on the name Jacob? It is impossible to say. The text says, God is Jacob's adversary.

In any case, when the man saw that he did not prevail against Jacob, he struck him on the hip socket, throwing Jacob's hip out of joint. Despite this, Jacob will not let him go without receiving a blessing. Is this a dream of his father Isaac and a desire for forgiveness and cleansing? The man accedes. 'What is your name?' 'Jacob.' Then the man said, 'You shall no longer be called Jacob, but Israel, for you have striven with God and with humans, and have prevailed'.

Jacob pleaded, 'Tell me your name'. The enigmatic response is, 'Why is it that you ask my name?' And there Jacob was blessed. Jacob emerged from the encounter overcome. 'For I have seen God face to face and yet my life is preserved.' He called the place Penuel. The sun rose upon him as he passed Penuel, limping because of his hip. Crossing the river, he went to meet his twin brother, Esau, who ran to meet him, kissed him and embraced him as they both wept. So the story ends with grace and reconciliation.

I share two of my own conclusions about this story. Jacob is astonished he has seen God face to face and lived. But the face he saw was a human face. He is told, 'You have striven with God and with humans and have prevailed'. I would reshape that sentence to read, 'You have striven with humans, and therefore God, and have prevailed'. The mystery of God's presence is buried in the human. The new name that Jacob receives, Israel, turns him back to his people as their representative leader. He and they together are one flesh.

So when Jacob asks for the name of his opponent, the response is rhetorical, even amused and ironical, 'Why is it that you ask my name? Is it not already given or to be found in "Israel"?' There will be no other way to seek out the trace of God. For all metaphysical quests for God are like the smell of old cigars in unventilated rooms, evocative of possibility, but in the end only smoke and insubstantiality.

I learned this in the dark days after Janet's death, as I prayed and wept over my loss. It was the memory of what we had been together, flesh and bone, real things, that helped me admit a new journey across the river having faced all I feared. And there on the other side, inexplicably, beyond my powers to explain, I was met and embraced, and invited to continue my journey, damaged though I was.

What have I found in the desert then, these last weeks? I found a company of people in whom the same questions as my own flicker and glow. I do not expect my answer to be yours. But in our time, integrity demands that we journey into the true wilderness, which is ourselves, and find there waiting that touchstone against which all is measured, that turns us back to ourselves. It is not without cost. There is a price to be paid.

So this Rock is a symbol for me of the Christ, that crystal through which true light is refracted and reaches out to guide our feet on the way. A life that makes transparent to us the source of our questing. Tolstoy wrote that 'God is that which makes it possible for us to say Yes to life'. If that is true, then God came to me anew in the form of my wife, Janet, and it is through her that I came to rediscover a faith, vital enough to give me life again. I would like to share with you, Helen, my own loved passage from *Markings*:

> What I ask for is unreasonable: that life shall have a meaning
> What I strive for is impossible: that my life shall acquire a
> meaning.
> But absurd or not, and it is absurd, beyond reason I say 'yes'.[27]

So why did I come to Uluru? It was what saying Yes required. What has it meant? Let me be enigmatic. I close with a story. It may help to explain my story more fully.

The story of Badger and Snifter

Badger the wisest of dogs, the sage of Labradors, trotted through the fern gully. Behind him snuffling, bounding this way and that came Snifter, he of enormous energy, abundant enthusiasms and dubious parentage. Badger kept an eye on his young charge, whose concentration span was of the thickness of a fresh smell.

They passed beneath towering ferns, and huge Mountain Ash. Soon they came upon the stream at the bottom of the gully and set off along the nearest side. The banks on either side grew steeper. Filtered sunlight dappled the water and flickered off the abundant green ferns.

Badger stopped suddenly at a very sharp bark. He looked across the stream. There, beyond all expectation, was Snifter looking bewildered.

'What are you doing over there?' called out Badger.

'Looking at you, Badger', said Snifter unhelpfully.

'No, I mean, what are you doing on the wrong side of the stream?'

'Standing here, Badger', responded Snifter.

Badger gave up. 'Come back over here, Snifter', commanded Badger in his most impressive voice.

Badger heard Snifter listing his options. 'I can't jump, because it's too far. I can't fly, because dogs don't have wings. I can't swim, because the water is too deep and swift. I can't dig under, because the stream flows over rock.'

'What must I do, Badger?' he cried. 'I cannot get back to you.'

Badger sighed. 'Snifter, you must go back the way you came. Find the place you crossed over to the other side, I expect it was a log, and come back to this side. Have you got that?'

'Yes', said Snifter, and set off at great speed in the wrong direction. Some stiff verbal comments from Badger stopped him and sheepishly (if dogs can be sheepish, while remaining doggish), he turned, raced off and disappeared from sight.

Moments later, tongue hanging out, his sides heaving, he was beside Badger.

'What have you learned, Snifter?' said Badger sternly.

'To get home, Badger, you must go back the way you have come.'

'Yes.'

'You must return to what you did not understand the first time.'

'Yes.'

'You must trust that you can cross over again to find the way you must go.'

'Yes.'

'You must listen to what you are told.'

'Well done, Snifter', said Badger.

'Badger, I have a question.'

'How do you find your way?'

Badger trotted a little further up the path to a vantage point and stopped. 'Look through the trees, Snifter, what do you see?'

'The tip of a mountain.'

Badger nodded. 'Keep that in view and take each path that brings you closer to the mountain. That is the way home.'

'It is hard to see it often, isn't it Badger?'

'Yes.'

'So you may have to go back again to what you know before you forgot what you know.'

Badger sighed, 'Yes, Snifter!'

Snifter nodded, then looked around. 'So where are we now, Badger?' There was no reply. Badger had disappeared from sight. Snifter, nose to the ground, set off in all directions at once.'

Vizard, watching Standfast, discerned the effort he had made to lift his narrative into a less sombre mood. Helen Wales observed him with moist eyes, grateful and calm. Daniel patted the storyteller on the knee. 'Your story speaks to me of the Rabbinic word. "God is the between when each is fully present to the other". I say thank you for your story for you and I are one in heart.' There were murmurs of agreement around the room.

Then all eyes turned as one to look at Archie Marshall. The small carpenter shrugged. 'When the world asks for help, who am I to refuse?' Appreciative grins spread around the room. The next offering would be something quite different.

Chapter 9

Archie Marshall

'It's difficult', began Archie, 'for a boy of the Western Suburbs to talk in public. Not to talk. To talk in public. Most of my life at home or in school I was told to shut up. What an invitation this is. To talk without interruption. Of course, working folk don't go into much explaining. We act. We respond. We do things. A lot of thinking means a pain in the head and nothing changed. I learned this from my gran, who brought me up. There are two kinds of people who can't be trusted to speak the truth, politicians and journalists, because they never have to live out the consequences of what they say. Every Footscray kid knows that.'

❖ ❖ ❖

Archie and the wisdom of his Grandma

My gran came through a depression alone, after her husband was gassed in the First World War. She raised my mother and my Uncle Bill through really tough times, collecting bad vegetables and rotten fruit behind the stalls at the old market, when the money she earned by cleaning and washing ran out too soon.

When my mum died having me, she took me in. 'You look after him', my dad said, 'I will go north, get work and send you money on a regular basis'. Gran told me when I grew up that she didn't believe it would happen. She didn't much take to my dad even after the wedding. But for five years, money came fairly regularly.

One day it stopped coming. Gran sniffed, 'Just as I expected'. Three years later, a policeman came to the door. 'Mrs Ratlow?' Gran nodded. 'Can I come in?' So he was ushered inside. There we learned that my dad had been killed in a tractor accident three years before. It had taken them all that time to find us. But there was an unexpected benefit. Dad had taken out an insurance policy on his life, 300 pounds. So we bought a small cottage.

All of those years, I listened to gran. To her wise words. It came down to two pieces of advice 'Trust the world. Something will turn up'. And 'trust yourself'. I went to the Footscray Tech, became apprenticed to a carpenter, and soon after got a job with a firm where I stayed until I was married and Joan and I moved to Oakleigh. But I always lived by that advice. 'Trust the world, trust yourself'. For despite what life dishes up, there is a kind of rough justice to it all.

The story of Blue Streak and rough justice

Take Spider McCann. He was my best mate. As cheeky as I was. One of the teachers, Mr Cairn, 'Ghengis' Cairn to us, took an instant dislike to Spider. He persecuted him, taking every chance to humiliate him publicly. Spider copped more detentions than all of us together. But Spider took it without complaint. I never understood how until Spider confided in me one day as we walked home after a shared detention.

Mr Cairn had one love in his life, a greyhound called Blue Streak. This beast had won an impressive string of races. Of late, however, he had failed to perform up to his earlier promise. What 'Ghengis' didn't know was that on Saturday nights, Spider worked at the dog track helping put the greyhounds into their starting boxes. Whenever Blue Streak was racing, Spider put him into his box. Just before the race, for the handlers often had to stay with the dogs, Spider would reach down (here Archie began to grin) and hold Blue Streak by the genitals.

Under such circumstances, he never lived up to his name, for reasons which can be appreciated, at least in the first seconds of the race. By then, he had lost all chance of winning. It was worth it, said Spider, even at the risk of being caught, because he had both owner and dog by the short hairs. Best of all 'Ghengis' didn't even know it. So a rough justice you could say.

That is the way it is. Three months ago, the boss of the firm I had worked for over twenty years called me in. 'We have to let you go, Archie', he said. I felt like a decrepit budgerigar. Twenty bloody years and all I get is 'We have to let you go, Archie'. He was too frightened to say they were 'downsizing'. With my height I would have had him for longitudinal vilification. So retrenched, with my super package delivered, I sat at home for a month, so sorry for myself that Joan said she thought she might have to have me put down.

'Archie', she said. 'We are going on a trip.' So we booked for this tour. A week later I had a call from an old friend at a nearby timber yard. 'Archie', he said. 'We want you to come and work for us as Yard Supervisor'. I was over the moon. So we prepared for our trip. Four days before we were to leave, my mother-in-law, who makes a lemon look frivolous, had a turn. What else! 'I can't go', said Joan. 'I have to look after her.' 'Why can't you tell her we have to let her go', I said. Not a wise response under the circumstances. In the end, Joan insisted

I come alone. So I did. Not without protest. But I start work when I go home so I decided to take the chance for a special kind of holiday.

The story of the demise of the Saints

These events which turn your world topsy-turvey, taught me again that you have to trust that if one door shuts, another opens. I remember the time I told Sister Josephine exactly that. I'm not a religious man, but being a carpenter - perhaps that's a religious vocation - I often did small jobs on the side.

Near our house in Oakleigh was a convent with huge grounds. Some of the local lads broke several palings off the back fence, sneaked into the nuns' showers, and put crystals in the shower heads. Red and green and blue. They were beautiful. The next morning Charlie Hogan, who lives closer to the convent than me, said it was the first time he'd heard the nuns' chorus. 'Would I fix up the back fence for them?' So I did. That began a long friendship with the nuns and particularly Sister Jo. I did a lot of work for them over the years.

One Saturday morning, Sister Jo came round to thank me and we had a cuppa and got talking and she told me about what happened when Vatican II took place. I thought VAT II was a whisky, but it was a ecumenical - I think that's how you say it - gathering which changed the rules or something. In the convent where Sister Jo was at the time, they decided to get rid of the statues in and around the convent. Too many people watching them all the time, I reckon.

So they pulled them down, loaded them in a trailer, and in the dead of night drove to a nearby lake. There they got an old boat, rowed to the centre of the lake and unloaded the statues. Horrors! They floated. What to do? They rowed back to shore, collected as many rocks as they could, found a torch and set off to bomb the saints. 'Imagine', said Sister Jo, 'this furtive band rowing round the lake despatching the saints with salvos of rocks, all by the light of a feeble torch!'

Sister Jo was laughing with tears running down her cheeks, but she was crying at the same time. 'It's alright', I said. 'When the old is done, the new will come. Something will turn up.' She looked at me, I like to think, fondly. 'Thank you, Archie', she said, 'you turned up for us when we needed you.' Charlie Hogan told me later that the Order had to close and sell the convent because nobody wanted to be nuns any more. When the convent was sold, I was away visiting my mother-in-law with Joan. The nuns moved away and I lost touch.

The Bomber returns

Many years later, I received a call from Footscray Hospital. Gran had been found wandering in the street in dressing-gown and slippers, her walking stick in one hand, selling tickets in a chook raffle to support the Bulldogs. Archie paused. The mighty Dogs, of course, are the Footscray Football Club, and Gran had supported them for years! [28]

She had approached one bloke waiting for a bus and badgered him to buy a ticket. 'Sorry, love', he said kindly, 'I'm a Collingwood supporter'. Whereupon Gran set to with her walking stick shouting all the time Treason! Treason!

It was clear she had lost her marbles. Alzheimers Disease it was. She needed to leave her home and be put in a hospice or some other place where she could be looked after. We didn't know what to do. Inquiries were fruitless. Available places were too expensive. I felt helpless. It was at this time, there was a knock on the door. I opened it and there was Sister Jo. She was grey, tired and stooped. But the twinkle was still there. 'Don't worry, Archie', she said. 'Something will turn up, and here I am.' She had been moved to Footscray, ran a hospice there for the elderly, and once a week visited the hospital. She had been introduced to Gran, found out her relationship to me and came right over.

We moved Gran into the hospice a week later. She didn't want to go, of course, because 'it was filled with old people'. She was eighty-two at the time, but we settled her in. I visited her regularly until she died. There was a moment during one visit when she seemed to recover her sense of where and who she was. She looked at me sternly. 'Archie', she said, 'why aren't you at work?' 'I'm here to visit you in your new room.' 'It's OK Gran', I said. 'It will be alright here. You taught me to trust the world, remember.' She looked at me gravely. 'You are quite right, Archie', you can.' Then she leaned towards me earnestly. 'Except when it's run by 'Pie supporters!'

I knew she was gone from us, but I laughed and patted her hand. 'There is no need to worry, Gran', I said. 'Sister Jo is a Bomber.' And I laughed and cried at the same time, just as Sister Jo had years ago in my kitchen, when she told me about bombing the saints. And for the same reason. We were both saying goodbye to that which we loved, whose life's end took our world to this point with them. With Sister Jo it was 'the Church' as she had known it; with me it was Gran who was 'family' to me all of my life.

I thought a lot about life then. Joan said to me one day, 'Archie you have become grave. That's not you. If you go on like that you'll end in one'. She was right, but I had to work it out.

The story of the wet paint

I don't have anything to offer that's profound. I do what I can, and help out where I can. Once I was doing some painting for Mrs Fidgett. When I left at the end of the day, the paint was still wet. 'Now don't touch it', I warned her, 'as it will be spoiled'. Later her husband came home from the pub a little wobbly, and, of course, put his hand on the wet paint, leaving a clear imprint. Next morning, I was met by a distressed Mrs Fidgett. 'Archie', she said, 'I want to show you where my husband put his hand last night.' 'There's no need for that Mrs Fidgett', I said, 'just a cup of tea and a biscuit will do me.'

When the laughter died out around the group, Archie with a characteristic bob of his head, responded, 'It's an old joke, I know, but it's reassuring to share old jokes when you feel sad'.

The story of lamps and tables

Take the time when one of my mates 'Bones' Lassiter bought an old table at a local fete. He came around the next day all excited. 'Archie, I've got this old table with marvellous carved legs. I want you to turn the legs into lamp stands for me. You know, polished up and made to look arresting.' Strange word 'arresting' for 'Bones'. In his case, it usually had other meanings. So I did.

Not long after this incident, Mrs Forbes whose husband runs a shoe factory, rings me up. 'Mr Marshall', she says, 'I have been fortunate enough to acquire at an antique auction some wonderful marble figures. If I leave them in the out-of-doors, they will not resist the pollution which is destroying of all genuine marble. So I have decided to use them as a base for a table to go in the conservatory sun room. Would you be able to make such a table for me?'

Who am I to judge? I say to myself. I do the job well and they feel great. And I get work turning tables into statuesque lamps and statues into tables.

Then there was the time I did some remodelling in the Stock Market building. There was all these blokes rushing around in suits. They would all wait until a bell rang and off they went like greyhounds after the drag on Saturday night. As slippery as rats up a drainpipe. The only difference I could see is that greyhounds don't have middles. I imagine that every now and then one of them runs fast enough to clamp his jaws on the lure. And when he gets there what does he get but a mouthful of mouldy old rabbit. I decided I would rather be with Spider holding on to Blue Streak. At least that was fun.

The story of snags and foul up

It all has to do with how you look at things, doesn't it? I remember how I was asked to help them get tables out at a convention run by the Rotary Club. It was a warm afternoon and we put the tables outside under the verandah of the reception place. The organiser was the local bank manager. Everything had to be just right. Chalk marks where the tables were to stand. Flowers on the table. Place names for everyone. 'It is important, Archie', he says, 'to ensure that the right groups mix with each other.' 'Yes, Mr Payne', I said, not quite understanding what he meant. So the guests arrive and they are having drinks. Mr Payne is watching the proceedings through a crack in the door. I'm working, lifting glasses and crockery on to a bench.

Suddenly, there is a great gust of wind, as can happen in Footscray. All of the place names, serviettes and a few other items are blown off the tables across into the crowd. Mr Payne becomes frantic. 'A total SNAFU', he moans. 'SNAFU?' I'd never heard the word SNAFU. One of the hired staff is bending over fit to burst. 'Snags and foul up, Archie', he says. 'Snags and Fowl up', I say to myself, 'they must be having a barbecue'. So I continued without concern. I learned later what they meant. But it all has to do with how you view it I decided. You can do your job and know what you are doing without having to pretend that you are someone else, or that the way things are is not the way they really are.

The story of the unrecognised legs

I heard a story once about a farm worker who came to the city. On the way, he found a purse by the side of the road with a lot of money in it. When he got to the city, he went into a big store and bought himself a multi-coloured pair of trousers with bright red braces, which were all the fashion, and matching shoes. Off to the pub, where he drank more than he should have.

On the way back to the farm, he became sleepy and so lay down and went to sleep in the middle of the road. Shortly afterwards, a car came along. The driver stopped the car and shouted out, 'Get your legs off the road or I'll run over them'. The farm worker sat up, looked down at his legs, which he didn't recognise because they were encased in multi-coloured trews and bright shoes. 'Drive on', he shouted back, 'they don't belong to me.' [29]

If you try to be other than you are, you can get cut off at the socks, believe me. So I asked myself, 'Archie, what do you want'. The answer was, 'what I've got'. I like sitting around with Joan, having a cuppa with my mates, going to the footy, doing my job as best I can, and helping out where people have a need. Gran used to say, 'Archie, you're lucky, you can turn your hand to anything', and she was right. It's a good life I have. Not great, not important, but satisfying. I take it as it comes. I trust it. You could even say I celebrate it. You can do a lot worse than that.

Spider McCann philosophises

Of course, I haven't made a lot of money. Just before coming up here, I bumped into old Spider in the street. Now Spider has made a lot of money, selling second-hand cars. So we sat down for a bit of a chat in the *Travellers Arms*. 'I hear you are rich now, Spider', I said. 'What's it like being rich?' Spider grinned. 'Archie, it's like this. When I started out, we didn't have much as you know. But the business began to grow. One day, my accountant comes to me and says - You are making some money, Spider. It would be good to spend some for tax purposes. So I say to the missus 'Is there anything you want?'. 'Yes', she says, 'I am always embarrassed going to the loo in the backyard.' We had an outside loo as you remember. 'I would like one in the house.' So it was done.

A year or so later, my accountant comes to me with the same suggestion. So I ask the missus again. 'I would like', she said, 'an outdoor barbecue area where we can entertain. Everyone has them these days'. So it was done. 'Now, Archie', Spider goes on, 'let me tell you the difference between being poor and rich. When we were poor, we ate in the house and went to the loo in the backyard. Now we are rich, we go to the loo in the house and eat in the backyard.' Spider laughed so much he knocked over his beer. A great character is Spider, I can tell you.

Meself, I'm not much good at stories. But there is one that I can tell that says what I believe. I heard it when I was still at school and I remember it to this day.

The story of the discontented cat

Once there was a cat who was dissatisfied with his life. The main reason was that he was constantly being chased by dogs. One day, the cat encountered a magician, who listened to his tale of woe. 'What do you want?', the magician asked. 'Turn me into a dog', said the cat. For weeks the cat enjoyed the life of a dog. His food was brought to him. He could go on walks untroubled. Mostly he slept in the sun. That is until one day he walked through a wood. Without warning, a tiger sprang from the bushes and swiped him with a murderous paw. Badly wounded, the dog managed to escape. It was some time before his wounds healed.

When they had done so, he sought out the magician. 'I'm fed up with being a dog. It has many advantages, but it is a high-risk venture when tigers exist. Make me a tiger.' So the magician agreed and lo! he was a tiger. Being a tiger was best of all. No more threats from enemies. Being the biggest and best was exhilarating. In this state, he lived many happy years. But one day, while moving through the jungle, he was confronted with death. Looking up, he saw a man with a rifle pointing at him. There was a loud report and a thud as a bullet entered his chest. The pain was excruciating. He turned and ran, knowing that his very life was at stake. But escape he did. The wound was deep, the healing painful and slow. His anger and frustration returned.

So he sought out the magician again. 'Magician', the tiger said, 'I have travelled many miles and learned many things. For the sake of my life and my true contentment, make me a cat again.' And this the magician did. It was as a cat, which he should have been all along, that, despite the annoyance of being chased by dogs, he lived out his life in peace and contentment.[30]

So these are some of the things I have puzzled over. Complaining doesn't help. You have to get on with it. I have been missing Joan these last weeks. Last night, I sent her a map of our journey to this place with little arrows and comments, like 'Here is Uluru', with a little arrow, 'Here are the Emu Walk Apartments', and a cross 'Here I am'.

Ian Standfast smiled inwardly. 'Yes, here you are, Archie, all of you, together in one place. Blessed are the pure in heart. You will always find yourself "here", Archie, because you take yourself everywhere you go, without holding back, or wanting more than you have.'

There was more conversation following Archie's offering. There was an engaging frankness about the little man that created an openness in response. 'You seem so content, Archie', said Jane wistfully. 'If you had a wish right now, what would you ask for?' 'You mean apart from having Joan here?' Jane nodded. Archie thought for a moment. 'I would choose that I always have the laugh on my side.' Jane laughed. 'You've got it, Archie, you've got it.'

'Does Uluru have any special significance for you, Archie?', asked Lila. Archie cocked his head to one side. 'You mean religiously? I can't say yes or no because I don't know what it would mean to be religious as different from living every day with thankfulness. I can say that being here has been terrific. I have seen the stars brighter than I have ever seen them. I have breathed fresher air that I have breathed before. I have seen further than I have ever seen. I have felt strangely excited every day, anticipating new discoveries, and I have heard stories that are comforting to me in a strange kind of way.

I expected to be melancholic without Joan, but, while I have missed her presence, I feel included in the way I do at home when we sit down for a chat and a cuppa. It has been like that all the way. New and unexpected things that somehow fit snugly into what you always knew or thought you knew.

Uluru itself is too big for me to fit into anything. Sometimes when I am working with different woods, with that wonderful variety of Australian timbers that is just breathtaking, I remind myself that all this variety is gathered together by the word 'tree'. So I suppose what gathers us all together in this place is 'Uluru'. It is the reason for all that we share together. I can't say more than that.'

Uncharacteristically, Archie seemed troubled for a moment. 'I don't have the words to say what I mean, but I guess it doesn't matter.' He looked around, and the familiar cheerful grin returned. 'We have had some bonzer cups of tea.'

Chapter 10

Alan Vizard

'Some announcements before I begin.' Alan Vizard gathered some papers together. 'Weather reports indicate we will be able to leave tomorrow as planned, although there are some flooded stretches of road. The cloud will lift and the rain cease overnight. No further rain is expected for the next four days. So tonight we pack up in order to be ready to start about 7.00 tomorrow morning.'

Further details followed, with several questions and comments around the room related to the early departure time, mostly of a good-natured kind. At last all were satisfied and the company turned its attention to Alan Vizard. He was surprised to discover he was a little self-conscious. The role-change from organiser to participant, left him feeling vulnerable, even defenceless. He cleared his throat nervously and began to speak.

Alan Vizard tells his story

Some of you are already aware of my story from conversations we have had on the way here. A university career focused on literature, history, philosophy and Fosters lager - a not uncommon undergraduate curriculum. Then a Dip. Ed. and various teaching posts, two up country, and the last at a school in the western suburbs of Melbourne. In between, for two years, I travelled overseas and across the top of Australia. When I began teaching at Yarraville, part choice, part necessity, since the Education Department did not take kindly to peripatetic employees, I had resolved, even resigned myself, to being a teacher all my life.

Over four years at Yarraville, I became increasingly restless. The conventional wisdom denotes it a developmental crisis, not quite mid-life, but getting close. There were a lot of factors involved, external and internal, and not all of them conscious. But what swung the balance and led to my resignation was a trigger event that brought all my unfocused discontent into a moment of irrevocable decision.

I had in one of my classes a young Vietnamese student, son of a couple who had come to this country as refugees. The school itself had many different ethnic groups, and a significant percentage of kids from working class Australian families. An explosive mix. Ng was precociously gifted. He had highly developed musical talents, topped the class in sciences as well as humanities, and was a better than average middle distance runner. Unfailingly cheerful, he was a delight to teach.

He shared my own love of poetry and drama and was conspicuous in the school musical *The King and I*. Every teacher will tell you what hard work teaching is. To have even one student who has a love of learning is a great boon. This delight of mine was the reason I think that the consensus slowly grew that Ng was my favourite. In a school of that kind, where bullying was rampant, such a judgment could be fatal.

I remember the incident as if it were yesterday. I was looking out of the window of a second floor classroom at the students playing in the school yard during lunchtime. Ng was by himself, reading in the sun and chewing on an apple. As I watched, five figures converged on the unsuspecting reader.

It was over before I could react in any useful way. Boots, fists, a baseball bat. Then the five figures ran away in different directions leaving a body on the black asphalt. Screams were rising from the schoolyard. Even from where I was I could see the blood. Ng was taken to hospital, a smashed nose, two fractured ribs, a broken arm, lacerations and cuts to his face and body.

I was sickened and furious and despairing. I had spent four years with these kids, for I recognised all of the attackers. I had preached peace, taught as well as I could, the greatest insights of the human race that give us dignity and ennoble our spirits - and all for nothing. The jungle prevailed. I understood Ivan Karamazov's lament well. Evil does exist. Evil is deep in the hearts of human beings, and why it should be so and how we deal with it was quite beyond my powers of comprehension.

I visited Ng's parents. Simple, honest folk bewildered and distressed. I visited Ng in hospital. It was over for him. Not because of the physical battering. Something deeper, more fundamental. The light had gone out of his eyes. Hope had been extinguished. Fourteen years old and his spirit was broken, perhaps for ever.

I wanted vengeance. I marched on the Head and demanded retribution for the perpetrators of this crime. The Head placated me. Proper procedures. Must protect the good name of the school. Keep it out of the press. Momentary aberration. Look at the record of the school. Perhaps Ng provoked it, who can say? I knew that nothing would happen apart from a mild rebuke. Here was the bureaucratic mind, frightened and defensive, moving to lessen the damage and to smooth everything over. I lost my temper, swept everything off his desk, ranted and raved, and left slamming his door with such fury that a picture of the school opposite the door fell from the hook and glass smashed over the carpet of the foyer.

Ng's family took him away. My days were numbered. The Union helped with the negotiations. A deal was struck. I left quietly with a reasonable remuneration. I had a publicly acceptable reason for going when all along I was inwardly resolved to go anyway. That was the irony of it. My friends poured sympathy upon me. But it was wasted. I was free I thought. Except for a nameless guilt for which I could give no explanation; I felt responsible somehow. I have had the same feeling when I have seen drunken Aborigines brawling in the streets of Alice, or being thrown legless into paddy wagons. It was dark night of the soul time.

The road of choices

In a novel by Morris West, there is a dialogue between the Ambassador (the name of the novel) and the Zen counsellor, Muso Soseki. A parable is shared which tells of a traveller who sets off on a journey in hope, but who becomes poor and old as the journey continues. At last he feels abandoned, untouched by compassion, overcome with guilt. There is no life worth living left. But the counsellor offers another possible end to the parable:[31]

> ...Our traveller cannot go back; there is nothing to urge him forward. But, without desire, he continues walking. By the side of the road he sees an image of the Buddha, of the Goddess Kwannon, of Rai-jin the thunder god, a fumiejesu perhaps, or even the Great Bear of the Ainu people. It is a dead thing of wood, or stone, or baked clay, which for our traveller has no meaning. But because he is a man, he knows the image has a meaning for other men: an expression of their need and their desire for enlightenment, harmony and elevation above the self. He stops by the image which has no meaning for him. He recites a prayer in whose efficacy he does not believe: 'If there be forgiveness, forgive.
> 'If there be tomorrow, grant me a hope in it: and if there be these things, but not for me, give me the patience to endure the not having.'
> 'And how will I know if the prayer is answered?'
> 'When you have the courage to live without an answer.'

'But if I have no courage?'
'Then you will walk just a little further along the road and
you will come to a habitation of men.'
'How can I be sure of that?'
'Because where there are images, there are always men'
'And then?'
'Then you will see what the Lord Buddha saw: an old man, a
sick man, a dead man, and a man with a shaven head who has
no home. And then you will say, "None of these is more
fortunate than I, so why should I complain?" And then you
will either accept to live again in the habitation of men or
you will join the homeless one and continue on the road.
And so, either way, your prayer will be answered and there
will be a beginning of light and a desire for more light.'
'And forgiveness? Who forgives me for what I have done?'
'The dead man whom you bury, the sick man whom you
succour, the old man whom you support, the homeless one
whose loneliness you share.'
'And the image?'
'Is still an image of the Unknown and the Unknowable who
may one day choose to enlighten you - for the All
Enlightened One has pity on mankind.'

It became clear to me in this time of questioning that if there was
an answer for me, it was to be found in the religious dimension of
human experience, almost certainly on the way to somewhere. I have
a great love of *Canterbury Tales*. Where could I go to seek an answer?
What pilgrimage could I undertake that would bring me into 'a
beginning of light and a desire for more light'? So Pilgrim Tours was
born. I fled into the desert, for cleansing, for a fresh start, in response
to a summons, into the presence of God, perhaps towards the
immovable Rock whose influence spreads over us even now. I felt as
if I

had set sail on another ocean
without star or compass
going where the argument leads.
Shattering the certainties
of centuries.

It was as if I had begun a second life quest, Ian, which is not yet at
a terminus. Socrates had been my guide in the first phase. 'The
unreflective life is not worth living.' But it is the Buddhist riposte
that guides the second phase. 'The unlived life is not worth reflecting
on.' When youthful idealism is shattered, you have to search through
the debris to find materials with which to begin building again.

I had lived within that envelope of law, ritual, custom and myth that nurtures most of us into some kind of human identity. But when you see it as socially constructed, humanly contrived and manipulated, then something else strikes you. That you have been sealed off from the natural world. You are no longer sensitive to or responsive to its rhythms. You do not hear the deep beat of the earth's heart; you do not stand naked before the stars and the immensity of the universe, but live smog-shrouded in habitats squeezed dry of the juices that give life to the body. Perhaps that is why I instinctively turned to the desert.

This desert ocean upon which we sail does shatter old certainties or, at least, gives rise to new possibilities. You learn out here that reasons are only reasons. They are not even truths, although they masquerade as truths often enough. You are brought to question what you really know. Think on this story for a moment.

The story of the king with two sons

There was a great king once who had two sons he loved very much. One a scholar, a kind warm-hearted young man, the king kept by him at court, partly because the young prince was not a warrior or an administrator, and partly because he greatly enjoyed the lad's discourse, the easy closeness they shared. The other son, also much loved, was a great warrior, a good and just administrator, the perfect choice for general to lead the king's army. But the king and his son rarely spoke, rarely shared their hearts, were rarely easy or close.

Yet the king believed the son understood, believed that their silences contained the same deep and rich understanding he shared with the other son, that the looks that did pass between them were full of unspoken affection, that nothing needed to be said.

Then one day, out of jealousy, out of envy, anger and disenchantment, the warrior son led a rebellion against his father. Without the king's knowledge, the scholar went forth to appeal to his brother, but in a rage the warrior son slew him as the focus of all his wrath and disappointment.

The king wept when he heard the news. He raged, he stormed, he did not leave his apartment for days. When he did come forth, he assembled his royal bodyguard, took his great sword and seven mighty spears and his fierce battle lions and rode out to meet his son. 'What will you do?', the king's advisers asked as they charged into battle. 'I know', said the king. 'What', his advisers asked, 'will you do?'. And the king, even as his son's army came into view said, 'I already know what I will do but I do not know what it is yet'.

What did the king do? He stopped his chariot. His arm was raised ready to cast, holding a great spear. He was in mid-charge. But he stopped and he stopped his army. He walked across to his son and forgave him. And his son killed his father with his sword.

The king knew, but the son did not yet know what he truly knew until his father lay dead before him. We discover by going through it.[32] We know more than we can tell, and we only find words for the deep truths that run in us when we commit ourselves to action.

The hidden words

You may have seen one of those puzzles that are printed in magazines. All of these letters are jumbled together on a grid, say about twenty by twenty squares. If you look hard enough, you will find words hidden in the mass, sometimes up and down, sometimes across, sometimes on angles. You will find words that are unsuspected by the designers also if you look at the letters and make French or German or Indonesian words.

There are endless possibilities for words. But they are only words because we call them so. It is a humanly contrived world we live in. Experience teaches it is a world patterned on subjection and domination. It is the endless play of our imaginations and creativity that brings forth the universe we inhabit. Out here in the desert, I have learned that the fundamentalisms paraded as truths are only one possible reading of the letters, as subject to time and relativity as the physical universe. There is no absolute standpoint. We never escape the net of language.

Language is our gift and our fate and with it we build castles in the sky in which we live. We cannot escape the relative, provisional nature of what we see and do, nor escape the temptation to turn our relative view into an absolute one.

That, I think was the radical dimension in the ministry of Jesus. He pointed to the envelope and named it for what it was. Not the intention of God, but the creation of human beings, who, once having exercised their creativity, then absolutised their creation and protected it as divinely prescribed. A disease of all religions and all societies. For every human world created is built by including some people and excluding others. We know we are in because we can point to those who are out.

Then Jesus comes along and says 'in God's realm, those you cast out are welcomed in'. What you call God's will is only human will writ large. Culture should be for the sake of life, not life chopped, folded, bent and adjusted for the sake of culture. His execution was inevitable. Human beings cannot accept too much of reality because without our illusions we have to come back to what we do not wish to admit. We are mortal. We are creatures of a particular time and a particular place. And this is the cage we cannot escape. We seek freedom from our fate, and then limit ourselves by the marvellous illusions in which we live.

Here is the paradox the desert has opened up to me. The more we know about the universe, the more pointless it seems. The more we know about the human, the less human we become in our eyes. So the key lies not in the knowledge itself, or fashions in being human, or in symbols whether mathematical, social or religious, because inevitably the outcome is division and warfare. It is the relationship between the symbols that matter, that network of mutuality which is largely invisible, but is the true foundation of all we see.

The story of the clown and the fire

Let me explain that by reference to an incident. A story is told that a fire broke out in a theatre. One of the clowns came on stage to warn the audience. They thought it was part of the performance and applauded. He repeated his warning. They laughed even louder. That which was deadly serious was treated as a joke because the symbolism of the context had become confused. How is it possible in such circumstances for the people on each side of the stage - caught between reality and illusion - to encounter each other as persons who share a common fate?[33]

In a multi-cultural, multi-faith society, we must become one people who see beyond the clothes in which we dress that grant identity, to the common destiny we share. Integrity requires that we own our own name, our own time and place, our own tribe, and, at the same time, honour and include those who express their humanness differently.

There are times to see beneath the paint, the costumes, the colour of the skin of the human subject, who can only be human in a particular way, but is yet always my sister and my brother and myself. It has been a strange journey of discovery these last years as I have come back again and again to this Rock. I do not know what I expected. I had no personal god to pray to, no hope in an interventionist god, only a kind of hunger for transcendence, some way of looking at the human journey.

I remember Geoffrey Chaucer's retraction at the end of *Canterbury Tales* and his prayer for forgiveness and succour. How powerful that plea is, and how futile. In the twentieth century, we do not have such a view of the world, or ourselves or God that makes such an act of penitence credible. So I thought. But what has come to me has been surprising. I do not understand it fully. But I can give you the outline of it in a parable that is close to autobiography.

The story of the man who became a mountain

Once there was a man who came to a sacred place, a giant monolith, with a question on his lips. It was the same question each time he came, but it had different forms. 'Does life have meaning?' 'Is there grace?' 'Where shall forgiveness be found?' They were all forms of the one question: 'What am I?'.

The mountain gave no answer. Each year he came. Each year the answer was the same. Each year he knew the mountain better. He recognised its crags and seams, its crevices and ridges, in all its moods and forms. The mountain was living. He talked with others about the mountain. They saw other things he did not see, wondrous things, strange to his ears, but he realised quite possible.

Then one year, he fell ill with a fever and could not make the trip to the desert. As he lay in his bed, his temperature high, there grew in his mind an image of the mountain. He saw it as he always had, yet sharper and deeper and richer and more mysterious than ever. 'Why', he said to himself, 'the mountain has come to me.' Later, it occurred to him that all the mountain meant was inside him, and the more he thought about it, the more marvellous it became. He could turn at any time and have communion with the deep silence of the holy place. He could enter into hidden caverns and visit secret water-holes. He was renewed, because he had visited the mountain, which was now within.

He did not return to the mountain for many years. He had no need to do so. He had gone one step further in his thinking. Even if the mountain was destroyed, it would not matter. He no longer sought the answer to his questions outside his own experience. He travelled within, that unexplored territory of his own being, a journey that led him on to unexpected discoveries.

One day, however, the image of the mountain began to fade. It became more and more indistinct. Just as night comes in the desert and obscures the mountain, so a darkness descended. For him no image of the mountain remained. But he was not disturbed. For the memory of the mountain remained. As if a promise had been made that said nothing will ever change with me, even if you change. He remembered how he had visited the mountain year after year and it was always there. It had been there for centuries and would be for centuries more, immutable, unchanging, eternal. There was peace in the old man's heart. He knew that somehow the mountain had claimed him. It and he were one creation, in an inner communion that defied time and place.

Sitting in the sun one day, now old and near the end of his time, he saw the sun glint on a small rock. Picking it up, he saw that it was made of the same substance as the mountain. It was as if a bird had lifted a small crumbling piece from the mother rock and dropped it at his feet. Holding it in his hand, he felt its warmth and comfort. A small boy, seeing his concentration, ran over. 'What do you see, old man?', he asked, full of curiosity. The old man smiled. 'I see myself.' 'What are you then, old man?' The old man looked into the young face. 'I am a mountain', he said, 'who has always been waiting for you to ask me that question.'

Vizard looked around the silent group of listeners. 'It is an old question, is it not? And its answer lies in another question asked long ago: who do you say I am? I am still seeking to understand what I know but cannot tell. In the tours I have run, I have found many pilgrims like me, who have come into the desert to find an answer. I have come to believe that no-one, who has come earnestly seeking and with a genuine hunger, has gone home with an empty heart. It is my hope that this tour will have afforded you your opportunity to ask your question, and then in the silence that follows, hear your answer, whatever it may be.'

Outside, the sun had gone. The group did not move for some time. Then Helen Wales struck a match to the candle on the centre coffee table. The light spread its warm glow throughout the room. Helen looked up at Archie. 'What about another bonzer cup of tea?' 'Helen', said Archie, 'who could ask for more?'

Chapter 11

The return

The day was clear but overcast as the bus pulled away from the Emu Walk apartments. It had not taken much time to pack and gather the travellers together. Each had helped the other; breakfast dishes had been washed and dried with dispatch, so that only minutes after 7 o'clock they were on their way.

The Desert seemed renewed, flowers flashing yellow, red and blue as they passed, the trees refreshed by the heavy rains of the last two days. A brisk wind still hurried across the sand dunes but inside the mini-bus, the heater had taken the chill out of the atmosphere. Here and there, some pools of water were seen, but the sealed road assured that there was no impediment to their journey. Lila spotted a small mob of kangaroos in the distance and pointed excitedly.

Otherwise, the same featureless pattern greeted their gaze, sand dunes running into the distance covered sparsely with saltbush and mimosa scrub. Small trees could be seen. At one point, Vizard pointed to a distant clump. 'Bloodwoods', he said. 'That means there is water underneath somewhere.'

Behind them, the cloud still obscured the top of Uluru, but sun sparkled off its sides. The colour of the Rock to the eye was orange streaked with darker brown where shadows were cast from ridges on the flanks of the sandstone. They watched it as it began to grow smaller. From time to time, comments were shared, but mostly the passengers seemed immersed in their own thoughts. The Rock diminished in size as they drove on.

At nine thirty, they stopped for morning tea, but soon after were on their way. Vizard watched them through the rear vision mirror. The morning tea had brightened them up. They were chatting to each other, some in serious conversation, Archie telling jokes and leading a small group in a game of observation of what could be seen from the windows of the bus.

Nipper

'What has the trip meant to them?' thought Vizard. For a citizen of
the Rock like Nipper, there was a clear view of the relatedness of all
that he experienced. His was a unified world in which the law
moderated all that he saw and did. His guardianship of the Rock gave
his life focus and meaning. It was a world that was seamless, rich and
subtle in the interaction between earth, seasons, human beings and
directions, a timeless present in which meaning glittered off every
grain of sand and small sandstone ridge.

Vizard remembered attending a ritual dance with Nipper's people.
He had watched the young boys apply the ochre, white, red and yellow,
to their bodies. They slipped into the centre to begin their dance and
at that moment they became the spirit of the animal they portrayed,
emu, rock wallaby, snake. It was uncanny. Each beat of the foot
reconnected them again to the earth, thud, thud, thud, quick precise
movements, a total immersion in their dream time identity. 'All of
our theories and explanations distance us from a primal sense of
participation like that', thought Vizard.

After the dance, he had seen how carefully the paint was removed,
how there emerged boys no different from boys of their age anywhere
in the world. Yet profoundly different. For the spirit of the Earth
breathed through them as no other. For Nipper and his people, as
long as their culture remained intact, the universe was seamless and
unbroken. But who could say whether the ancient wisdom would
prevail. A McDonald's hamburger came to mind. The boys had taken
off their paint and been given take-away food as a reward. Which
world was real? Which world would prevail?

Lila

Vizard's gaze shifted to Lila. Lila also lived in two, perhaps three,
worlds. Hers was still a world filled with spirit beings, an eternal cosmic
struggle between good and evil. It was a world caught in an endless
repetition of the same patterns, in which the daily pattern of events
was intruded into by forces that must be engaged and placated.

Such a world view also was complex and subtle. The peculiarly
Balinese response had been to invent an artistic mode of being in
which beauty and harmony were brought to birth in every daily action.
All of life was ritualised, the earth, the sky, fire, water, air, not just
physical elements of a material world, but the living spirits whose
progeny was Art, transmogrified by devotion and will into beauty.

The soul stealers were at work here also. The computer with its
logical, abstract reasoning, was as threatening to the Balinese mind as
any Rhanga. The literal always seemed to conquer the metaphoric.
How was it possible for the artistic sensibility of the Balinese people

to resist the flood of tourists and the rising tide of waste and cynicism they brought with them? Village girls, driven by poverty, brought into the brothels to serve the appetites of those who, having no beauty of their own, sought only to destroy the beauty of others.

Uluru meant many things to many people. Had Lila found here a reassurance that the god of the mountain was everywhere the same, and everywhere filled with love for all that is created? Vizard had seen, as they left the Emu Walk apartments in the garden, a small basket filled with rice and flowers. What prayers had been offered? What hope expressed? Lila lived at a crossroad between two cultures, between the roles and status of village wife and computer controller, between a mystical world of spirits and the disenchanted world of the silicon chip. How would she choose? What would become of her people? How would they survive the great profanation?

Archie

Archie Marshall shouted and clapped his hands. Vizard smiled. Archie, like Nipper and Lila, had something of the child about him. There was in him a fundamental trust of the world. Archie made no great claims. He projected for himself no significant status. But Archie, like many others unsung, were the salt of the earth. Vizard recalled a line of Tolkein's which he couldn't place - 'the little people turn the wheels of the world, while the eyes of the great are elsewhere'.

With Archie, what you saw was what you got. He had made sharing a cup of tea and eating a biscuit a sacramental act, as if the very commonness of things was the source of its claim to be sacred. In Archie, there was no metaphysical dimension, no abstract reflection about origins, no developed sense of fate or deep appreciation of suffering. Just the simplest of gifts, a glad and thankful heart and an unfailing desire for companionship and sharing.

When Archie, with a cup of tea in his hand, told Joan of his trip to the Rock, what would he say? 'I encountered the demon of the mountain and overthrew it?' More likely, 'Gee it was big, luv'. Of all of them, Archie had least problem with the question of identity. He knew who he was and accepted it without complaint or regret. He was a man without guile, or envy or desire to cut others down. How seductive it was to wish you were as sure as Archie.

But there was for some of the others no chance of a second naivete. The strokes that had felled Ng had shattered any illusion Vizard had about the perfectibility of the world. Or any inevitability about progress. It was not Nature 'red in tooth and claw' which worried him, but the humiliation of spirit, the crushing of human dignity, the drop by drop torture that wore away self-esteem, the impoverishment of the lives of countless people by those whose world was certain and untroubled. Archie bore the gift of community with him, but he had no personal word for someone like Daniel Levi.

Daniel

Daniel was happily engaged with Jane, Vizard saw, smiling and at ease. But the deep sense of moral outrage he carried, would always be with him. The resonance of injustice from the past sounded in his soul like a gong whose deep tolling had travelled down the centuries to this time. It was the gift of his people to be the moral conscience of the world through their own victimisation.

Vizard knew that the Jewish community still wrestled with the holocaust. Some had emerged from the death camps believing more firmly. Others had experienced there the death of God so fundamental that if God existed they would spit in his face given the chance. The intangible, inexplicable occurrence of faith. How was it to be explained?

For Daniel and his generation, the threat was two-fold. Anti-semitism flourished, as prolific as weeds that must yearly be rooted out of the same flower beds. But more serious than the external threat was the inner question of identity. 'If I forget you, O God, what can I be?' What ground of identity remains if God dies? The Torah has no authority, the rituals of redemption have no meaning, confession is an arrow fired into a void. No, the holocaust, both event and symbol, would not go away for Daniel's generation, Jew or not.

Vizard wondered what the visit to the holy mountain had meant for Daniel. Had he found there an imprint, some trace of the God who was the God of Abraham and Isaac and Jacob? Or had the breaking of the sea of injustice been so loud that he could not hear the still small voice? We are ethical creatures who want an answer to the question of evil. Theodicy remains the greatest obstacle in a century in which we cannot pretend, though some try, that the holocausts of Europe and Africa and China and Russia and Latin America did not occur. Still, the mountain was there, and the cloud, and the question.

Jane

Jane Orchard shared something of the same dilemma. The problem of identity for her was focused in the gender issue, but included all those other dimensions with which Daniel wrestled - psychological, sociological and religious. Jane's generation also experienced the death of the old gods. The template had been cast aside. Her age group had decided to invent themselves, gone into free-fall. But if one tries to live through broken symbols, how can one escape contradiction?

'Madonna', a public rehearsal of nihilism offered as a realistic human option.

In the end, it had to run out of fuel and discover that illusion duplicated by illusion brings you back to the greatest illusion of all, that you have a self. If you live by illusion, you will fade into illusion. So Jane had asked the question squarely 'What is real?' 'What is human?' She was honest enough to know there were many possible answers. And that she had to decide for herself. Her temptation is, thought Vizard, to choose in terms of what she is not, for then again she is controlled by the others she most fears. Whatever answer she forges out of the fires of creation, let it be tempered by mutuality, not exclusion.

What then had Uluru been for Jane? A mirror, she had said, which reflected back to her that the answer was to be found in the life of the questioner. Vizard thought of the image of a tattooed man on which each tattoo told a story. Jane had to tell her own story, find words and images and symbols that opened up a highway she could walk with integrity. Would the burden of choice be too heavy, the absence of guide rails so dangerous that on a slippery patch through the fog, she and her generation would fall into a chasm? Time would tell.

Colin

Colin Freeman was the most interesting of them all. A gifted scientist and, Vizard had learned, an accomplished musician. For him the future was an encounter with mystery. He had discovered the truth of Haldane's observation that the universe is not only stranger than we can imagine, but stranger than we could possibly imagine. How does one deal with the knowledge that our brains create the reality we see, and even more frightening, that it is the 'learned' structure in the brain that is critical in all that we perceive.

Human intelligence may discern that the physical world can largely be described by mathematical codes. But this is not the only way to describe the world. Are there other possible analogs by which, using different language, we would encounter another reality or realities, equally rational, equally possible, equally quantifiable by scientific method? This leads on in ever reducing circles back to a relativist point, a black hole of thought, one step short of nothing.

Even here, science, in its own realm, encounters a threshold, which a singularity such as a black hole presents, which cannot be crossed. There are mysteries that cannot be compared with anything we know. The disclosive power of science lives through the breath of language.

Uluru was its own kind of singularity metaphorically, thought Vizard. How can one engage God in language, when language itself has no power to describe that which is ineffable? Human beings do not possess language so much as being possessed by language itself. When the universe ceases to be a problem to be solved and becomes a mystery to be encountered and entered into, all explanations fail. Here subject meets subject. That which is Other confronts us. We must make some response to it. Is it communion or participation or homage? What is the word that best describes an appropriate response to that which defies language?

Freeman had moved from science as a disclosure venture to realising that it was a transformative commitment. Who then would name this mystery? Vizard thought of the old saw that the real skill of astronomers was not discovering new stars, but being able to find out their names. Exactly. So to be a scientist was to enter a process of becoming, rather than commentating on things as they are. By whatever standard, the irony was that being a scientist was now an act of faith in itself.

Helen

Perhaps Helen Wales knew more about the nature of that mystery than Colin. At least she was able to say 'yes' to life in the presence of death. It was a 'yes' not just of courage in the presence of inevitability, nor the triumph of hope over experience as Dr Johnson would have it. It was a profound response to the mystery of life itself and its claim upon her. Vizard wondered what his response would be to the certain knowledge of the manner and form of his own death. Somewhere a choice had to be made, which took one into the void as into the arms of God.

Uluru, whatever else it did, brought me to some kind of decision, thought Vizard. A demand for authenticity, one's own inescapable life, a singularity, however time-bound and short-lived, brought into the presence of eternity. It was the eye of faith that saw the true relationship between time and eternity, not eternity in time, but time in eternity. That way of seeing our life made all the difference.

Was Helen different, Vizard mused, as a result of this pilgrimage? Did she find an answer to her heart's need? There was about her a peacefulness that he had seen also in Ian Standfast. Not a resignation, but a full-hearted acceptance that left no place for self-pity. A readiness, even a secret joy.

There was a stir of envy in Vizard as he watched her. As if she knew, really knew, that Death was one of the names of God. The suggestion shocked him for a moment. He was not yet prepared to consider what that might mean. He had a sense that Helen was going home with relief. She had hazarded this venture within her meagre span of time and found some kind of treasure, of that he was convinced.

He hoped, one day when his turn came, he would understand what it was as well as she.

Ian

Ian Standfast came into his mind's eye. He felt very close to the old man. Setting off on his final journey, not of discovery but of relinquishment. The depth of the old man's faith had been moving. He had reminded Vizard of Anselm's words:

> Lord, I do not attempt to comprehend your sublimity because my intellect is not at all equal to such a task. But I yearn to understand some measure of your truth which my heart believes and loves. For I do not understand in order to believe, but I believe in order to understand. For I believe even this: that I shall not understand unless I believe.

'Vizard', he had said, 'I have no confession to make outside of Christ's claim on me. I have no other story to tell, but the narrative of God's care. If you ask me what it means to believe, all I can offer is the story of my life. It is a poor enough testimony, but it is all I have to give as validation of all that I have been and done. You remember Chaucer's plea:

> Send me grace to bewail my sins and to study the salvation of my soul: and grant me the grace of true penitence, confession and satisfaction ...so that I might be one of those that at the day of judgment shall be saved.

Hardly any of that language means anything to me any more, Vizard, but it does express something of my own search for wholeness. God grant me a straight way and a peaceful end.'

Alan

Not surprisingly, Vizard had noticed how often Helen sought out Standfast's company. They spoke the same language and listened to the same music. 'God speed old man', he said, 'God speed.'
'What have I learned this trip', Vizard asked of himself, 'in the visit to Uluru?' Neville Coghill's comments on Chaucer's pilgrims spoke in his mind:

> It is the concise portrait of an entire nation, high and low, old and young, male and female, lay and clerical, learned and ignorant, rogue and righteous, land and sea, town and country, but without extremes... The most noticeable thing ... their normality. [34]

He was surprised to recall also Dryden's words: 'Tis sufficient to say …. that here is God's plenty'. [35]

'The curse of a literary education', thought Vizard. 'God's plenty! I don't believe in some Other out there, so God's plenty is a way of placing the being and action of God within us. If language will suffice at all.'

'Is it possible', he wondered, 'in all its variety, to accept this small company as the microcosm of an Australia-that-is-coming-to-be? A nation struggling to give expression to the hope that is in it, a raft on a sea of meaning that finds commerce between its differences and certainties a reason for strength and purpose? What was lacking in the wider community', Vizard thought, 'was a sense of a common purpose'. No nation could develop as one people without significant common goals. Nor could it persist and thrive without significant common action. Just as Uluru had focused the pilgrimage of this small community, so a common story was needed that called forth a sense of destiny in all those who called themselves Australian.

There was need for a unifying symbol, a sustaining metaphor that spun out into mythic possibilities. In this story a love of the land, a respect for difference and diversity, a capacity for silence, an acknowledgment of distance, a common language of love, all these were needed. Vizard reflected a moment. 'If these pilgrims are noticeable for their normality, what could I call up from their lives?'

The gifts of Uluru

Nipper, the gift of a respect for a fundamental order; Daniel, a commitment to manifest justice; Archie, an unshakeable trust in life's intentionality; Jane, the gift of new birth; Colin, a humble recognition of mystery; Helen, an open acceptance of life's unrepeatable chance; Ian, faith, hope and love; Lila, beauty, balance and harmony. And myself, the hunger for something more, the lure of the horizon.

Could all these together, the gifts of ordinary people, be the means of bringing into being a truly unified community? Could such gifts be the source of a truly religious vision of a land renewed? Yes, Uluru, means many things to many people. Yet it, itself, is a singularity beyond all description. Perhaps it is there to point us to our destiny.

Some kilometres further on, Vizard slowed as the sign 'Floodway' appeared, and then braked as it became clear that water was flowing across the road. With Colin and Daniel, he went forward to investigate. The others watched anxiously. 'It looks like it is subsiding. We will break for an early lunch.' Food and drink were produced from the bus's storage compartments and the company sat down together in the sun and shared their meal together.

After lunch, Jane walked a little off the track and began to gather stones together. Archie joined her, then Colin and in short order, the whole company became involved, seeking out rocks to add to the pile. The cairn grew higher and higher. At last rocks became scarce and energy waned. 'Time to move on', said Standfast.

They looked back along the way they had come. The road stretched back to the horizon which remained flat and unbroken. Vizard engaged the gears and slowly the bus entered into the gully, swayed as the water pressed its sides, coughed and grunted, and then a heart-stopping pause before it emerged triumphantly out of the waters, climbed the side of the floodway and made the road once more. They moved on, picking up speed. The cairn disappeared from sight. Faint singing could be heard across the desert. No-one looked back.

Section II

Narrative theology: some reflections

Chapter 12

A new path to the waterfall

We live in a time when people are seeking out story-tellers to recover again the wisdom of the race. The reasons are complex. One writer offers this perspective:

> We can only re-tell and live by the stories we have read or heard. We live our lives through texts. They may be read, or chanted, or experienced electronically, or come to us, like the murmurings of our mothers, telling us what conventions demand. Whatever their form or medium, these stories have formed us all; they are what we must use to make new fictions, new narratives. [36]

Here the claim is made that stories provide a fundamental structure within human experience, giving shape to what we know and can know. The conclusion is clear. The quality of our life is significantly influenced by the kind of stories we tell. Those stories we internalise most deeply confirm us in who we are and what we might become. We become the story we tell.

This fascination with narrative is no new thing; it has a long intellectual history. Aristotle in his *Poetics* and Augustine in his *Confessions* wrestled with the nature of narrative and the way in which time and place are given form through the telling of stories. As we do today.

Some definitions

Some definition of words is helpful here since already narrative and story have been used as if they are interchangeable. In a discussion on *Experience and Narrative Inquiry*, Connelly and Clandinin argue that narrative is both phenomenon and method.[37] They choose to use 'story' to refer to phenomenon and 'narrative' to method, as a mode of inquiry. People, they suggest, tell stories and live storied lives. Those who collect stories and tell them compose them into a narrative pattern.

This distinction can be illustrated by reference to the first eleven chapters of this book. Many stories are told by the characters. The whole is woven into a coherent narrative. The relationship between story and narrative is therefore very close, for it would be appropriate to say Uluru Journey is a story, as we commonly use the word. But for purposes of distinction the definitions above, guided by the ideas of phenomenon and method, are useful, and necessary for clarification.

Story is also a catch-all word for a number of forms of story, myth, saga, legend, fable and so on. It is helpful, therefore, on occasions to pause to identify the kind of story being told for each operates under its own requirements and has a unique contribution to make. The most comprehensive of these is myth, and a case can be made for regarding myth as a larger word than story. To call a myth a story can domesticate it alarmingly. Whatever distinctions or definitions used, however, there is no debate about the claim that all forms of 'story' in their own way are about the human experience of living in this world, however we chose to define 'world'.

The destruction of sacred story

At this point in history, it is the perception of what we mean by world that is one of the breaking points in our understanding of narrative. I can illustrate what this means by relating an incident that occurred in a class I was teaching some years ago. During a discussion on myth and symbol, I read a Maori myth that originally set out to explain human failure to achieve immortality. It was an account taken from a book *Wahine Toa Women of Maori Myth* by two New Zealand women, Robyn Kabukiwa and Patricia Grace. The story was as follows:

Hine-nui-te-Po is the one who looks after the spirits of people when they pass to the underworld after death. Maui-tikitiki-a-Tarange had performed many miraculous feats and his greatness was to be the conquering of death and making man immortal. To do this he had to enter Hine-nui-te-Po by way of her birth passage, pass through her body, eat her heart and emerge from her mouth. He took his friends, the birds, with him to watch. Once there Maui tried various disguises before settling on a lizard form. He began his journey through Hine-nui-te-Po's legs but the fantail could not hold back his laughter at the ludicrous sight. This woke Hine-nui-te-Po who crushed Maui between her legs. Thus was the balance kept. [38]

Immediately upon completion of the reading, there was a hostile reaction from one woman in the class. 'I utterly reject this story. It is an incitement to rape. To me it is a story about rape and the defilement of women.'

This response is a possible one if the myth is read sociologically. But from another standpoint, the response was not appropriate. The dilemma of living in a post-modern environment was opened up before us in a most arresting way. Joseph Campbell claimed that there are four functions of myth - a religious or mythical function, a cosmological function, a moral social function and a psychological function.[39] In each myth, the unity of these functions was taken for granted when they were first told. These were sacred stories with a heuristic purpose.

When such stories are told today, however, they are heard not as a unitive explanation of the world but rather as justification for patterns of domination and oppression. In the case of the Maori myth, of male oppression of the female. The sociological and psychological dimensions of the myth have broken away from the religious and cosmological. Operating in a socio-political context quite different from that of the primal cultures and the world views in which the stories were first told, myths have become autonomous and definitive in their own right as stories.

The consequence is that the stories no longer function as myths. The mythic consciousness they presume is no longer accessible, for, if not destroyed, it is no longer efficacious for the process of interpretation. We live in a disenchanted world. That which once was sacred is now de-constructed out of a secular orientation, and can no longer tell us of the wider, more comprehensive vision of human commerce and engagement myths were intended to convey. They are judged now to be fabulous accounts, in the original sense of fables, and therefore reflective of a false consciousness about the nature of the world.

This experience was a salutary one in my own understanding of the post- modern dilemma. I had chosen the myth to illustrate how many cultures have stories of the loss of immortality or eternal life, whether Greek, Hebrew or South Sea Islander myths. My intention was to explore the vision of the human situation these myths offered. In one stroke that intention was destroyed. For once the protest was acknowledged as valid, other possible interpretations could not be entertained. We had lost the mythic-poetic way of seeing the world in the deconstructed vision of a post-modern age.

Distinctions that could be made about the nature of language, whether literal or metaphoric, formal or ecstatic, actual or symbolic, practical or theoretical, inclusive or exclusive, integrative or transformative, were irrelevant. Even the motive of the story-tellers was unimportant. They were deceived as an examination of the undertext revealed. The myth was not politically correct. We had reached a terminus. And what we had was what we could see. No other worlds were acceptable. The rich fertile insights of the human imagination issuing forth in the form of myths had no currency, no continuing significance in the presence of the sense of violation expressed by the hearer of the story. We had reached an impasse because the justice of the protest could not be ignored.

The present age

It has been claimed that the myth of modernity is the story that kills story. In the ancient classic *The Book of the Thousand and One Nights* the plot evolves around the desire of the king to hear stories.[40] Scheherazade, the daughter of the Wasir, in order to save her life, goes on telling stories for a thousand and one nights. The king had put to death every other lover after his first night with her, but since Scheherazade did not complete her story at the end of each night, the king stayed his hand in order to learn how the story concluded. At last, the king realises he has fallen in love with her and the book ends happily.

If you take one step back and ask what is the primary intention of the author/s of *The Book of the Thousand and One Nights* you quickly realise that the setting is a device used to tell stories. Similarly, the journey to Canterbury was the supporting foundation, the structure enabling Chaucer's pilgrims to tell their stories in an acceptable environment of purpose and meaning.

In our day, however, the sub-text becomes dominant. Scheherazade uses stories as a device to deal with her powerlessness. Her stories are only a tactic, a stratagem in a fight for survival. The stories have no curative or transformative power in themselves. They become merely technical apparatus in a power struggle, the weapons of the weak who have no other resources with which to survive. The stories themselves cannot be the focus any more, for it is the political situation which conveys the true message of the book. The dominant can be rendered ineffectual. The weak overthrows the strong by use of story. In this reversal, the second 'story' kills the stories. Their lustre is dimmed, their light shut out.

The mythic consciousness was dealt a death blow during the age of reason and the growth of the scientific world view that followed. Now that the world view gained by the Enlightenment has itself fallen into disrepair, we have in a post-modern age only the utilitarian option. If it works, keep it. If it is economically, socially or psychologically viable, secure it. If it furthers the purpose of our group or sector or community, justify it. One of its outcomes is political correctness, which while advocating more just relationships, dangerously narrows the scope of human interactions possible, or at least the comprehensiveness of the stories that can be told.

The price is high. There is no chance of a united front, a holistic vision eludes us in an environment increasingly tribal. Perhaps that is why there is a desire to recover story as story. Its promise is the recovery of a unitive vision. But the source and ground of that vision is unclear.

The classical vision

There have broadly been in the common era according to Don Cupitt three visions of the world which have been determinative in the West. [41] The first of these, the classical vision, was theonomous. All of culture was directed to the praise of God who dispensed favours and responded to the prayers and supplications of the people. The world was an act of God, reflecting God's nature and shaped according to God's purposes. All that could be seen was God's work of art brought into being by God's powerful and creative word.

Human life, therefore, had a contemplative focus. People responded to nature and history as the theatre of God's self revelation. Such a view can be summed up in the metaphor of a downward arrow. All of life had this address from God at the top, then the church, rulers, authorities, both hereditary and elected, and ordinary people. The required response of ordinary humans was one of passive obedience. It was a static, ordered and predictable world. Human agents had little initiative except that of grateful and obedient response to the givenness of life.

The modern vision

The modern view of the world gradually subsumed the classical perspective. Its roots can be traced to medieval thinkers, but it grew to its strength and flowered through the 18th and 19th centuries. This period is often referred to as the Enlightenment, a time when, in juxtaposition with the Renaissance and the Reformation, an age of reason emerged. There sprang up a science based industrial culture. The universe was conceived as a machine operating according to inflexible laws available to our understanding through mathematical formula and empirical experimentation. By the exercise of reason, we might gain complete understanding and control of this world.

In *A Brief History of Time*, Stephen Hawking talks about discovering a complete theoretical explanation of the world. Hawking believes we are close to such an achievement, and concludes, 'if we find an answer, it would be the ultimate triumph of human reason - for then we would know the mind of God'. [42]

The Enlightenment was a time when not God but the human was the focus. The metaphor is an arrow moving horizontally out from the human subject who is the centre to an explanation of an objectified universe now subordinate to technology, mathematics, physics and the investigations of the human sciences. The vision of this world view, with its commitment to progress and evolutionary advance, permeates our world, even of economics, in its purist form of economic rationalism.

The post modern vision

In the twentieth century, an alternative vision of the world has appeared. Since it is in part a reaction to the sterility and failure of the modernist vision, it has been called post-modern. The breakdown of a rationalist view of the world with all of its assumptions of inevitable progress was hastened by two world wars, the holocaust, and the creation of the atomic bomb. This is what science, for all its achievements, has delivered under its promise of a new heaven and a new earth. An alternative view has begun to emerge with accompanying changes to social life and thought.

Both the classical God-centred vision and the human-centred vision of the Enlightenment sought to unify the world by focusing it around a centre, conceived in each case as a centre of understanding, power, control and self affirmation. The key idea of mastery was first enshrined in God. The 'death' of God gave birth to the sovereign self and the new centre was located in the aspirations of human beings.

But in the post-modern world, this centre has gone also. There has been a breakdown of a one centred universe into many centres. Deep shifts have occurred in the ground structures of human life and shared existence.

However post-modernism is defined or understood, it is in part a reaction to the abstraction in life and thought that characterised modernism. The 'dizziness of unending abstraction' had led, as Carl Jung remarked, to the bridge between dogma and the inner experience of the individual breaking down.

A further characteristic of the period of modernism was its attempt to develop a master narrative which gave a comprehensive and satisfying explanation of human nature and destiny. It was unitive and sought to contain all human endeavour within its embrace. It was also definitive and prescriptive which had the effect of hindering action and stifling variety. Its certainties were too overwhelming and in the end could not be sustained as its story broke down in a time of escalating pluralism.

Simone Weil was close to the spirit of the turn from metaphysical abstraction and its claim to certainty:

There is a God. There is no God. Where is the problem? I am quite sure that there is a God in the sense that I am sure my love is no illusion. I am quite sure there is no God in the sense that I am sure there is nothing which resembles what I can conceive when I say that word. [43]

It is in the context of this kind of general experience that there has been an emergence of narrative inquiry. Thomas Berry states it this way:

> It's all a question of story. We are in trouble just now because we do not have a good story. We are in between stories. The old story, the account of how the world came to be and how we fit into it is no longer effective. Yet we have not learned the new story. [44]

It is out of this social turmoil that new interest in narrative has emerged. Alongside this interest have appeared a variety of other attempts to think theologically that are focused on different centres of concern, such as feminist, liberation, ecological and cultural theologies. They are indicators of the break up of a unified vision of the world, and the rise of pluralism which characterises our present experience. The situation now is not so much that the centre cannot hold but that there are many centres which bid for a primary commitment.

In the disenchantment associated with the decline of a rational-metaphysical world view and its own decline as a creative force, there has been a recovery of the narrative-symbolic. The purpose of narrative has always been an awakening of the self. In the turn away from objective descriptions of reality and the accompanying objectification of human beings who came more and more to serve the industrial and technological environments created by a scientific world view, the offer present in narrative symbolic patterns is a recovery of a deeper sense of the human person and the depths out of which human life seeks to know itself.

However this development is welcomed, whether positively or negatively, the reality seems to be that the plausibility structures that supported the former modernist vision of the world have broken down. That is part explanation for the dilemmas confronting institutional structures whether health, education, welfare, the church, or systems of public order. Present institutional systems were shaped and conceived in the 18th and 19th centuries and no longer seem either inevitable or appropriate to present experience.

Of the major consequences of this shift, two are worth identifying. There is a widespread disappearance of respect for institutional authority. In addition, there has developed a determined dismantling of all sacred claims so that in an age of mass media, all truth assertions are reduced to advertisement and publicity. The outcome is propaganda.

The theologian Walter Kasper writes:

...mass atheism, a phenomenon unparalleled in past history
...regards the practical, if not theoretical denial of God or at
least indifference to belief in God as by far the most
plausible attitude to take. As a result, theology has been
stripped of its power to speak to people and to communicate
with them. There are now no generally accepted images,
symbols, concepts and categories with which it can make
itself understood. This crisis in the presuppositions for
understanding talk about God is the real crisis of present-day
theology. [45]

Why narrative?

Some years ago when in Africa, I set off with a friend to visit the
Victoria Falls, product of the mighty Zambesi river and one of the
natural wonders of the world. So great are the falls that spray begins
to descend upon you even before the falls are in sight. On the day we
sought to make our way to the viewing places overlooking the falls, a
sign had been erected indicating that the usual path we sought to
follow was blocked. We had to seek a new path to the waterfall. In
order to do that we had to divert through undergrowth and trees
filled with chattering monkeys. Finding a new path had its hazards.

In much the same way for us, many traditional paths to religious
meaning are no longer available to take us to the goal of our quest.
With all the hazards involved, we have to seek new paths to the waterfall.

One of those paths is the narrative-symbolic. The viability of
striking out in this direction is advanced by Alasdair MacIntyre in the
following way.[46]

1. Intelligible human action is narrative in form. We are significance-
   seeking and meaning-making creatures who communicate
   primarily in words structured into narrative.
2. Human life has a fundamentally narrative shape. We constantly
   seek to discover purpose and meaning in what we do by rehearsing
   the story of our lives.
3. Humans are story-telling animals. From this perspective, the gift
   that sustains, and creates human cultures is our capacity to tell
   stories.
4. People place their lives and arguments in narrative histories. One
   illustration of the truth of this claim is the fascination people have
   for family histories and genealogies.
5. Communities and traditions receive their continuities through
   narrative histories. Abraham begat Isaac, Isaac begat Jacob, Jacob
   begat . . . In each case, the stories, myths and legends associated

with those named become formative and determinative in particular communities and within a Judaic-Christian tradition. Other communities and cultures name themselves through other narrative histories. But it is through stories that identity is conferred.

6. Faith development is marked by the construction and reconstruction of more adequate narratives and forms of narrative. In any living tradition, as stories are told and retold, they are reshaped, placed in different interpretative frames, and redirected to serve the need of the present age. The infinite vitality of primal stories is a continuing source of life to individuals and communities.

The conclusion to be drawn from MacIntyre's claims is that narrative is the fundamental source of identity. As Barbara Hardy has it, 'we dream in narrative, remember, anticipate, hope, despair, believe, doubt, plan, revise, criticise, construct, gossip, learn, hate and love in narrative'. [47]

Theological reflection in much of its formal statement has left little space for the contribution of narrative as the source of identity. It has been concerned to articulate and describe with precision the essence of that which is believed. The positive dimension of this concern for theological accuracy, as genuinely reflective of an authentic understanding of the church's tradition, has been the clarity with which the faith can be presented. It has sought to divide truth from error, and to overthrow the dark spell of superstition and wish fulfilment.

Increasingly, however, the formal theological deposit has been of less and less help as people struggle to make sense of their lives. In extracting the essence, the orange has been squeezed dry of vitality and sustenance. To change the image, a magnificent tree has grown out of rocky soil. But it only has one root which travels underground some forty metres to the water source that gives it life. If that root is cut, the whole tree dies, for it has no other way of finding nutrients to sustain its life. The tree has developed to its fullness too far away from the source of its life.

For many the theological descriptions that have given direction to past generations seem no longer vital enough to interpret their contemporary struggle to state what they believe. They prefer to seek understanding within a present communal context that gives them purpose and meaning. Here is the return to tribal identity, a facet of pluralism. They do not wish to be directed by descriptions of Christian existence that come into their experience from outside in language that does not communicate to their present search for direction. As Westerhoff affirms:

A metaphorical, poetic, symbolic, mythical relationship to God is always prior to any signative, conceptual, analytic

> explanation ... For too long we have attempted to
> understand reality solely through reason and have forgotten
> the importance of symbolic narrative, metaphor, and the
> sacred story. [48]

The temptation in this situation is to dismiss the gains of the Enlightenment as irrelevant to a post-modern world view as some do. Just as the classical vision gave way to the modernist vision, so the modernist vision capitulates to the post-modern world view.

The reality is that dimensions of all three visions - classical, modernist and post-modernist - intermingle. Within all of us a kaleidoscopic swirl of images keeps alive all possible options. Very few people live uncontaminated in one intact vision of the world. But we do have a feeling of what makes sense to us, and what does not. Things have to cohere, and our experience today is not so much a sense of integration as of disintegration. We search for more satisfying explanations than we have been given by past generations.

If the rational-metaphysical mode of doing theology was too much a reflection of the Enlightenment and led to obstruction and scepticism, so too the narrative-symbolic is easily co-opted to contemporary fashion and illusion. Even more, it can give birth to a form of subjectivism which is self indulgent and dishonest.

A proper relationship, therefore, is not one of placing rational metaphysical and narrative symbolic modes in unresolvable contradiction but to maintain a dialectical relationship between them. Each has its contribution to make that achieves a healthy balance, and enlarges options and possibilities available to both sides of the conversation.

As Brian Wicker points out, 'Metaphor ...raises questions that only analogy can answer, while conversely analogy can only answer questions that are raised in a metaphorical form.'[49] Even further, much of the ancient wisdom of the race is not available to us if we choose to cut off the narrative-symbolic. The religious insights of sages, prophets and teachers can only be made accessible if appropriated in their original form of story - whether myth, parable, legend, fable, saga, wisdom saying, proverbs or koan. In this is included the teaching of Jesus, who following the Rabbinic tradition of his time, taught in parable, poetic contrast, and with interpretative gesture.

The emergence of narrative theologies are driven partly because of a deep hunger to re-appropriate understandings of God, given originally in the narrative-symbolic form, which have been excised by the rational-metaphysical mode of reflection Also in part, the desire is to find ways of sharing and offering faith, that offer new paths to the waterfall because traditional paths seem blocked.

It is the readiness of theological communities to give recognition to this turn to the narrative-symbolic which is at issue. As has been argued above, some truths are only available to us through the narrative-symbolic mode of engagement. The over-emphasis on the precise statement of orthodox doctrine needs to be brought into collaborative endeavour with the life and struggle of local communities seeking to name themselves within the unique and pressing demands of their own context.

Perhaps the ironic perception of George Orwell is useful here. Orwell quoted Ecclesiastes 9:11:(K.J.V.)

> I returned and saw under the sun that the race is not to the swift, nor the battle to the strong, neither yet bread to the wise, nor yet riches to men of understanding, nor yet favour to men of skill; but time and chance happeneth to them all.

What this is really saying, suggested Orwell, is better understood in the following way:

> Objective considerations of contemporary phenomena compels the conclusion that success or failure in competitive activities exhibit no tendency to be commensurate with innate capacity, but that a considerable element of the unpredictable must invariably be taken into account. [50]

It is this kind of mystification that Orwell is attacking which is being resisted by those who turn away from dogmatic theology in a search for words that speak simply of God's reality.

Narrative seeks to return to the direct, first hand language of experience because the high value placed on intelligibility and rationality has drawn us away from language that helps in the practical verification of what believing means.

It is clear that if there is a sense of crisis within faith communities, much of it is because accustomed ways of living and expressing faith are breaking down. The crisis of the self is the crisis of the tradition that formed the self, and we are in a situation so unclear that we must call on the active imagination to offer hope where descriptive reason has fallen dumb.

Martin Buber tells the story of several yeshiva students found by their rabbi one day in the house of study, playing checkers when they should have been studying Talmud. Embarrassed, they returned immediately to their books. But the rabbi smiled and told them not to be ashamed, since they always should study the law wherever they found it.

So he asked if they knew the three rules of the game of checkers. Obviously, they assumed they knew what they were playing, but none would be so bold as to appear to teach the rabbi. Therefore, the rabbi, the master of Talmud, Kalshala and Zohar, rehearsed for them the rules of checkers. 'First' he said, 'one must not make two moves at once. Second, one must move only forward, not backward. And third, when one has reached the last row, then he may move wherever he likes. 'Such', he said, 'is what the Torah teaches' - and he left. [51]

However one interprets what is meant by the story, it offers the possibility of finding God's intention not just in a book but in community, not only in work but in play, not in that which is intentionally pursued alone but in that which is incidentally appropriated. Or in both intuition and intellect together. That is the elusive power of story. It teases us with possibility. The promise is clear. It is the creative imagination which can point us to where an ancient but forgotten way will open up anew, and lead us to the waterfall.

I said to the Almond Tree,
'Sister, speak to me of God'
And the Almond Tree blossomed. [52]

Chapter 13

The turn to narrative

Some years ago, I was involved in teaching a course on Story to Aboriginal and Islander people. Most came from tribal environments. The experience taught me that many assumptions we hold about narrative, influenced by literary and historical critical criteria, are not appropriate in primal cultures.

Tribal people live in the stories they tell. They do not see them as separated from their daily existence. The stories told, to my ear, sounded flat and mundane without serious attention to plot, character, continuity or any desire to increase the hearer's fascination by bringing the story to a climax. I would listen to a story and make little of it.

But to the students inside the mode of discourse there were mythological references, encoded levels of meaning, which defy easy description. The Aboriginal and Islander participants would respond enthusiastically, and refer in discussion to totem connections or tribal symbolism that resonated in them as they listened.

Conversation jumped over normal continuities with connections that only made sense if you understood the immediacy of contact with the land and its creatures and its story. Just as a handful of notes struck on a piano can, to the trained musician, bring to mind Bach and Beethoven, so the flat account of a mundane event could set ringing echoes of meaning that were deep and profoundly significant.

It is clear that the very ground of human consciousness is narrative fertile. Whether the form of the communication is written or oral, narrative has the power to open up our experience in revelatory ways. Texts or theological statements densely packed and encoded need story to release what is intended, or pointed to, or hidden, in what is stated intensively. Unlike primal cultures, who live out of stories, we need ways of finding our way back into truth by means of stories, because our world has become distanced from us by reflection and abstraction.

That step back into participation is possible because we are story-telling animals. The story itself is like one of those escalators in a large department store that carry us to another level of awareness filled with fresh delights. It is not just anecdote or illustration that is meant here, but something considerably more potent. We are talking about different levels of meaning.

It is salutary to be reminded that the best things can't be told and that the second best are easily misunderstood. We know more than we can tell, and stories give shape to that tacit awareness which evokes meaning and guides our behaviour. Of course, too much can be claimed for narrative. We are emerging from a time when too little has been admitted.

The turn to narrative follows many paths. It can be stated in academic language. Narrative is 'a crucial conceptual category for such matters as understanding issues of epistemology and methods of arguments depicting personal identity and displaying the content of Christian convictions'. [53] Or more simply. 'What stories ultimately satisfy is life's hunger for itself, its desire to exist, its desire to be turned on, its desire to be given form and made able to flow.' [54] But however we say it, we are story telling creatures. The turn to narrative occurs because in a time of confusion we have no other choice. Like Dick Whittington the bells sound and call us back. We return again to narrative in order to name our destiny.

Characteristics of Narrative Theology

So what does the turn to narrative involve? The following ten characteristics of Narrative Theology are not all that could be included but they indicate the territory, and ways of crossing it, that can be recognised in those writing in the field. The listing of these characteristics enables central assumptions to be declared about narrative itself.

1. Narrative gives priority to the mythic/poetic rather than the rational/metaphysical modes of discourse.

This claim should not be read to suggest that there is no reasonable element in the use of narrative. Narrative Theology has its own logic and follows structures which can be identified. Nor should it be read to infer that there is no knowledge dimension to story telling. Some ideas are accessible only in the form of myth or parable.

Reality itself, as Ricoeur claims, is re-described through metaphor. We are talking not about an inferior way of doing theology, but rather a different form of doing what is attempted in another way by the rational/metaphysical. It is to understand theoria as contemplation as the Eastern church does, not as a rational or comprehensible explanation as in the West.

It is not helpful to set the active imagination over against the work of descriptive reason. There is more inter-active engagement in the creative process between these ways of thinking than is normally recognised. And the mythic/symbolic is a way of thinking, amongst other things that can be claimed for it. What is being asserted here is a mode of theological reflection that has its own distinctive style and integrity.

2. Narrative is open to many levels of interpretation.
A simple example of this claim is the Prodigal Son. The endless interpretations of the story (is it the story of the Elder Brother? the Waiting Father?) indicate how continually fertile the parable form is. We draw fresh water from the same well whenever we visit it. The parable itself can be interpreted psychologically, sociologically, mythically, ethically or theologically, with infinite variety in each of these capacities.

When the question is raised of the parables, 'What did Jesus intend?', the answer may have less to do with what we declare to be true, or whether the parables unveil the meaning of the kingdom of God, than the evident outcome that they stir us again and again into new thought and action, precisely because they are unclear and open to interpretation.

3. Narrative employs indirect communication.
With all forms of metaphoric language we are enticed to think indirectly. Since we are seeking to make visible that which is not evident, it is inevitable that what is communicated points beyond itself. The literal mind of the scientist exploring what is 'evidently there' serves only to destroy meaning when applied to symbolic discourse.

The language of narrative is symbolic, indirect, metaphoric and multi-dimensional. It is imagery appropriate to addressing the category of mystery and cannot be seen as the means to solve the problem of God, or any other problem for that matter. What it offers is not for the resolution of problems but for the widening of vision and the evoking of faith, love and wonder.

4. Narrative creates community.
Stories can be told to many ages at the same time. Whether young or old, meaning can be appropriated at a level of understanding reached by each hearer. Stories told in a community, whether home or congregation, give rise to a common view of life, enable an open flow of communication, shape and re-inforce identity, and give rise to a sense of inclusion and intimacy. It is our stories that bind us together, and enable us to say 'this is who we are, this is what we believe, this is where we belong'.

5. Narrative affirms the concrete and the specific.

Stories are about something definite. Even when they operate in fantastic environments, in exotic worlds, or among alien or mythical people and creatures, they are about specific, tangible interchanges between place, time, and protagonists. We may not recognise details. These worlds, though the product of fertile imagination, are nonetheless real to us because what happens can be visualised.

It is the image, concrete, filled with the detail of everyday transactions, even if it is fighting dragons, that gives rise to thought and recognition. We can place ourselves in the story, whether as conqueror or victim, because it is concrete and specific. We cross over, explore, experience, and return again to ourselves enriched by the imaginative journey we have been invited to take.

6. Narrative requires that we suspend ethical judgment.

Stories can be told that are directed to arguing a moral point. Prudential wisdom is taught in this way in all cultures. But even the most explicit moral fable can lead to further questioning. If the boy who cried 'wolf' was eaten by the wolf in the end, was it entirely his fault? Perhaps he was practising behaviour he had observed in the adult world? Telling lies is not confined to children. Should adults allow children to be destroyed by their own immaturity? Why should a child be abandoned because he tells lies? Surely there are more appropriate ways of dealing with such a situation? And so on.

The alternative interpretation, the think-again imperative of stories, offers a chance to question iron-clad certainties, as well as re-affirm them upon reflection and consideration. The ability to suspend ethical judgment and to reason into different, perhaps more appropriate responses before acting, is one of the great gains of narrative reflection whether by case study, contemporary story, or inherited wisdom. Narrative reflection is a major tool in ethical development and moral instruction.

7. Narrative accepts the ambiguity of language.

If I pass a barber's shop and see a sign 'Five chairs working' I do not stop the car and rush into the shop to observe the miracle. I know it is shorthand for saying we have five barbers working at five chairs.

Advertising in our day, in its use of story, image, event and slogan, knows that the force of a communication is enhanced by ambiguous language, not reduced. For the ambiguous slogan can link the hearer or reader to other dimensions of their experience and thus strengthen by association the appeal of what is offered. As the Bank says to young home buyers 'You find the home. We'll come to the party'. It is in the ambiguity of language rather than its precision that narrative digs around, snuffles and smells, knowing that there is more to be uncovered by the undeclared than the defined and prescribed.

8. Narrative is unitive in style.
Attention has already been drawn to Joseph Campbell's claim of the unitive nature of myth, and its power to hold together psychology, sociology, religion and cosmology in a holistic way. Parable, by contrast, can be subversive, bringing about a disintegration of prevailing world views. But the end of parable is not permanent subversion but a return to a more encompassing holistic view. It is directed to drawing attention to the marginalised, the dispossessed and the victimised in order that their claims be heard and they be re-integrated into the dominant culture in a healing way.

The pattern here is one not of separation by distinction, analysis or reduction, but an encompassing intent that seeks to affirm what is universal and shared. Where differences are highlighted they are for the purpose of pointing beyond to a common fate or destiny. It is this inclusive intent which is most distinctive about the style of narrative.

9. Narrative honours direct experience.
To listen intently to a story is to be unavoidably present. Its impact is immediate and vivid. Here is first hand experience that may take some time to digest and understand. There is no escaping the task of processing the inner detonation yourself. By contrast, much that comes to us with logical consistency is second-hand, has been processed by others and sits uneasily with our present understanding and experience. Luther was right of course: 'Only a fool learns only from experience'. [55]

The very language we use presupposes a tradition, a social context, a communal indwelling. But it has often been here that the authority given to past descriptions of social reality have been used to discount and confine what only reflection upon our own immediate human struggle will tell us. In narrative, the dimension of direct personal engagement is made manifest. Its claim upon us for responsible and informed reflection arises out of that vast sea of possibility the narrative address gives us.

10. Narrative is provisional and searching.
In our day, much that comes to us from the past ages of the church's life has the weight not of truth but of propaganda. Part of the reason for this judgment is that in our age of mass media we are constantly being exhorted to buy and consume, much of it tacitly if not overtly, advocating a particular life style and philosophical orientation. On television, the offerings of earnest evangelists seem not so much a sincere offering of the gospel as just another consumer option with the same kind of claim to significant benefits by affiliation and gifts of money.

Because the world of story is multi-dimensional, open and properly subversive, it pushes us not to dogmatic certainties but provisional and searching conclusions. Many dedicated Christians today are asking, in a time when past formulations of the faith and the language in which it is expressed is no longer compelling, what can I believe?

The answer is not to be found by shouting louder or insisting upon commitment to prescriptions of obedience but by seeking through shared engagement a deeper appreciation of what we are striving to describe. In this redefinition, the stories we tell, the biblical stories, and the stories of searching people of other times, enable a process of existence clarification. We are pushed beyond regarding our present formulations as a deposit of truth to conceiving faith as a journey, a pilgrimage that takes us not into unshakeable certainties but to deeper and richer faith perceptions of God's generous presence in all of life.

The weakness of narrative reflection

These ten characteristics of narrative will serve to confirm in some readers the doubts they nurture about narrative theology. The revival of narrative has been criticised in many ways, including the charge that behind the interest in narrative are strong escapist tendencies.

Some of the criticisms raised deserve careful attention. In what follows, ten weaknesses attributed to narrative are identified. Perhaps they are more properly named as temptations which can be seriously resisted only when they are identified as temptations. Any way forward requires recognising their presence.

1. Fictional

Australian Aborigines who retain their mythical world view hold the belief that stories of the Dreaming are true. That is, they are given, and have the same weight in Aboriginal society as the Torah does in Judaism. When working with tribal Aborigines, I found it was necessary to draw a simple typology covering stories. Some stories are true. Some stories have truth in them. Some stories are false. Often a student would check a story by asking 'Is it true or did some one make it up?'

The idea that a made-up story was not true, because not actual, is not confined to primal cultures. We sometimes use the word fiction to describe what is untrue or made-up, in the sense of a lie, in our own culture. The resistance to products of the creative imagination has its roots in a scepticism about its contact with real events and therefore to history. So a common charge against narrative inquiry is that it is fictional, and therefore suspect, and by implication, untrue.

Such a view has not stopped Christians from the time of Jesus taking his parables as uniquely revelatory. Yet they are stories made up to convey to a particular audience truths which could not be communicated in any other way. The concern about narrative as fiction is not so much the form of communication but its content, and more importantly the use to which it is put. Propaganda is one illustration of how lies and distortion can be advanced as true, given control of the means of communication and a particular social context.

The argument here raises proper questions about particular narratives and the use made of them. But if we only accept that which is secured by custom and tradition, then transformed life and the possibilities inherent in a new vision will be denied us.

2. A-historical

Richard Niebuhr was strong in his conviction that the stories which guide faithful people today have their meaning only within an historical context.

'It remains true', wrote Niebuhr, 'that Christian faith cannot escape from partnership with history, however many other partners it may choose. With this it has been mated and to this its loyalty belongs, its union is as indestructible as that of reason and sense experience in the natural sciences.' [56]

Niebuhr goes on to raise a further question. 'But though this is true, the question remains: How can it be true? How can revelation mean both history and God?' [57]

We are dealing with complex matters here. But one answer Niebuhr gives to his own question is that what is true is communicated by story. The stories we tell define who we are. The bridge between the external world of historical account and the inner world of present conviction is by story. As Niebuhr argues, 'The history of the inner life can only be confessed by selves who speak of what happened to them in the community of other selves'. [58]

The unreplaceable parable of the life of Jesus remains determinative. But it becomes true for us by story, not just by the repetition of historical detail but by imaginative participation in the story as interpreted and lived by countless people. That story makes possible endless other stories. These stories ceased to be revelatory of Christian existence if they drive us away from the defining centre of the church's life, but that is not a necessary outcome. And without narrative, the external history of what God has done can make little contact with the inner dimensions of our lives. We grow by affirming a unity of these two realms of experience.

3. Subjective

Another charge levelled against narrative is that it lapses easily into a personal, subjective pattern. What happens to me becomes the dominant concern. Emotionalism replaces grace-filled reason. Contact is lost with the wider social context of a faith community that retains the integrity of the Christ event. A sense of social responsibility disappears because of a seductive fascination with my own needs and life journey.

What accompanies this preoccupation with the self is a dependence upon psychological processes, and the interpretative paradigms of psychology and sociology. Theological inquiry as a proper corrective to other patterns of interpretation has little or no influence on how stories are understood and owned. The danger can be detected in Cupitt's claim:

> I am the story I can tell about my own life, and the more
> artistically coherent and ethically satisfying the story I can
> tell the more emotionally fulfilled I shall feel. [59]

But it remains true that revelation is not revelation if it is not subjectively appropriated in some way, whether by the means of story, or creed or proposition. A profound inner conviction is necessary for anyone to claim faith. The test here is not whether it is subjective but whether it is appropriated individualistically, and is closed to the mediating and corrective influence of a community grounded in an authentic reading of the tradition.

4. Ideological

In a post-modern age, it has become increasingly evident that all stories are ideological in intent. No story is value free. The sub-text, which shapes a story's assumptions about social role, status and power configurations, illuminates the claim that all stories are ideological by nature. How does a story view the status of women or men? How does it view the poor and the rich? What does it say about racial difference? What assumptions about the ordering of society does it take for granted?

In the case of the use of the word 'God', what do the images or metaphors attached to the Divine say about 'God' or more importantly, about those who hold that image of God to be true. The pit of relativism opens up at our feet. Where is one to stand?

A moment of reflection leads to the conclusion that what is being said about the ideological intent of stories gains its force because the 'Master-narrative,' which once was taken for granted, has broken down. The Master-narrative was not free from the charge of ideological bias nor could it be. All human fabrications reflect the time and place from which they arise. But it advanced its claims as if it was bias free.

What we now see is that all stories must be open to scrutiny. They become less a reinforcement of established patterns than opportunities for more productive investigation of the many worlds available to us. It is as if we hear the old words in a new way. 'Let those who are without ideology cast the first stone!' As Ernest Gombrich reminds us '...there is no innocent eye .... The eye always comes ancient to its work'. [60]

5. Biblical distortion

There are two main streams with many subsidiaries running in the fields of biblical interpretation which relate inevitably with each other. One is the historical critical which has many different forms and outcomes. The other is the literary critical stream which also has many tributaries.

For some who fish in this second stream the historical ground or accuracy of the Scriptures is of only passing interest. Their claim is that we cannot know the full story of who wrote what, or with what intent. We cannot be sure which are the authentic words of Jesus, for example, and which are products of the early church put into the mouth of Jesus.

To be overly worried by historical veracity is to be diverted from what we can capture from the Scriptures as texts. They speak to us as they are. They say things to us that the original authors could never have envisaged. Let us then be free from guilt, and open ourselves to literary investigations in which imaginative reconstruction and free flowing interpretation can offer far more genuine food for faith than a self-consciously historical critical engagement with the Scriptures.

It is the separation of these two forms of biblical inquiry that worries critics who see the literary stream flowing out into a sea of error. The case for inter-relationship is well made.

Here the danger exists that if one option is used to deny all other possible avenues to truth, error and distortion will result. Just as the literary critical schools cannot claim a monopoly on biblical interpretation, neither should any other academe claim pre-eminence. We are at a time for collaborative dialogue, not competitive exclusion, in which the struggle to be responsible heirs of the tradition is shared and celebrated across many fields of inquiry. The literary critical school, which includes the narrative symbolic, is one important contributor to the total mosaic.

6. Truth claims

How are the truth claims inherent in story to be assessed? The argument here is that catechetical teaching, and the authority of the Magisterium, are constantly undermined by stories. Story is the enemy of dogmatics. Catechesis becomes diminished because the authority which lies behind what is taught is constantly questioned by story.

A cynicism is bred towards sacred things, as can be illustrated by the graffiti that appeared at a Sydney railway station. JESUS LIVES had been painted in large letters. Underneath in smaller lettering was the question 'Does this mean we don't get an Easter holiday?' The anecdote supports the charge that story can be the means of destroying faith possibilities. There is in the turn to narrative, critics claim, a constant leaching away of a common deposit central to Christian identity. Revelational claims are put aside. We descend into a dark night in which all authority is cast aside in the name of autonomy and freedom.

However, the force of the criticism is blunted by the realisation that a claim to absolute truth makes little or no sense when it in no way illumines daily life. Further, claims to absolute truth always appear clothed in the temporal language of a particular culture and are reflective of a particular time and place.

It is the refusal to accept any truth as absolute by decree that is found among the young. Claims to truth must be presented gently and provisionally so that there is freedom to explore the offer being made. Narrative has the kind of flexibility needed to allow investigation of what is or can become truth. It does not presuppose a right answer, but provokes the hearer to seek what truth may be. The defence of any citadel depends on being able to recognise who are friends and who are enemies.

7. Absolutist

A further charge laid against the mythical-poetic is that it seeks to escape criticism by placing itself above the normal canons of judgment. Its claims are beyond the balance and sifting which are applied to propositions and logical statements. Advocates of narrative claim 'this is the way it is'. Such a stance brooks no argument and permits no dialogue. The only option is to accept what is offered or reject its vision.

A mythical world view is comprehensive in its embrace. There is no half-way house. As a consequence, the narrative-symbolic can lead to irrational, unfalsifiable beliefs, that wreak havoc because they have no recognisable external checks on the excesses they contain. A tentative, even humble, approach to the pervasive mystery of life, is pushed aside by absolutist claims proffered in an arrogant and uncompromising way, which is destructive in the end of the very truth it claims to defend.

Such a criticism, however, is not confined to a narrative-symbolic pattern of thought. The rational-metaphysical paradigm is similarly susceptible to absolutist excesses. What lies behind the criticism is a recognition that human beings readily, if not inevitably, employ all truth-claims as a ground for self-justification. Ironically, it is the narrative-symbolic in its prophetic and parabolic modes, that breaks free from this bondage by its recurrent suspicion of all totalist claims.

8. Irrational.

The very form of narrative-symbolic inquiry makes it difficult for rational criteria to be applied in a completely satisfactory way. 'The heart has reasons' as Pascal observed 'that the reason knows not of.' Visions of human purpose and Divine interaction, which rise from the realm of the creative imagination, are not open to rational inquiry in the same way that other theological and dogmatic assertions are.

The disparity observed here has long been pursued in the art-science debate. Most people recognise that what is at issue is two equally viable ways of exploring reality, each with its distinct contribution, and each with its own limitations, appropriate to what it seeks to offer, display, describe, analyse, or celebrate. Since the debate is well known, it is only necessary here to affirm the autonomy of the narrative-symbolic as a different way of thinking, whose contribution cannot be diminished by judging it by what it is not.

Nor can it be assumed that, by definition, the irrational is always destructive and demonic. The beatitude bears witness. 'Blessed are the cracked, for they shall let in light.'

9. Romantic

This charge laid against the narrative-symbolic rests on the assumption that the forms of artistic endeavour blinds adherents to the way human life is lived. It has no capacity to undertake social analysis, identify its own complicity in corruption, and engage unjust socio-political structures.

The final outcome of a narrative-symbolic vision is an other-worldliness which has no redeeming word or positive contribution to social transformation. For the romantic oscillates between fantasy and melancholy, between unreality and cynicism. The real world loses focus, and becomes blurred by wish-fulfilment and escapist tendencies.

While this danger, like the others mentioned, is certainly there, it is a restricted view of the narrative-symbolic that does not see its genuinely prophetic and revolutionary possibilities. What has been transforming for abused women is the chance to tell their stories. Out of the telling of these stories has come new possibility, made more powerful by the linking with other stories of other women and other groups who are now empowered to make a difference.

Narrative has an extraordinary range. There are stories which unify. There are stories that subvert and destroy. There are personal stories. There are stories which speak about renewed social interactions. There are stories that talk about a new heaven and a new earth. There are stories that embody a romantic vision and a tragic vision, an ironic vision and a comic vision. The total range of the narrative-symbolic cannot be circumscribed readily. It has endless forms and unending inventiveness that make one dimensional judgments valueless.

10. Self-Indulgent

There remains one final charge against narrative that is deeply entrenched in the churches. Those who resort to story as a primary mode of communication are, it is argued, self-indulgent and prone to dishonesty. Behind the criticism is the conviction that narrative cannot embody hard thought and is prey always to sentiment and emotionalism. There is no critical objectivity about what is said. 'If it is my story, it cannot be judged by anyone else'. 'Our story cannot be subject to revision by outsiders because it is our story not theirs'. This refusal to allow the stories of a person, group, or community, to be questioned, means that distortion and dishonesty can flourish unchecked.

In a pluralistic society, characterised by tribal affiliations of various kinds, the dangers pointed to in this criticism have to be taken seriously. In the last few years, newspapers have been filled with the stories of religious sects who have been destroyed by a vision out of step with a common sense view of the world, and captive to the charismatic influence of leaders whose charisma had given illusory hope, which finally led to death and destruction.

Such outcomes are not inevitable, nor are they the outcome of a dependence on the narrative-symbolic, which can, if tied to an authentic tradition, save communities from the confusion and destruction mentioned above. Stories can be healing and redeeming. They can break the 'cover story' in which we are hiding and offer a wider horizon of meaning and significance.

As with the other nine attacks on narrative briefly identified, it is not inevitable that the dangers named will prevail over what is helpful and saving. They remind us of the temptations that assail those who seek a new way by means of the narrative symbolic. They should also serve as a reminder to those who operate exclusively out of the rational-metaphysical mode, that there are similar temptations that assail that mode of theological inquiry as well.

Narrative and the confessional stance

The present discussion concerning narrative theology arises out of a need for a unitive vision, in a time when the old stories have ceased to be persuasive. Mythic structures have broken down, including those which are enshrined in liturgies and the ritual practices of the church. The widespread search for more satisfying patterns of worship reflects a dissatisfaction with established ways of offering our life to God as believing communities.

But the way in which this search is approached reflects fundamental assumptions about our present world views. Something of the dilemma is illumined by the following anecdote. There is a story of three baseball umpires who were discussing their craft. The first one said, 'I call 'em as I see 'em'. The second umpire shook his head. 'I call 'em as they are'. The third umpire demurred. 'Until I call 'em they don't exist.'

Without wanting to stray too far into the debate about language, these three views are influential in how people respond to the present crisis of meaning in the West.

1. I call 'em as they are.

These are those who remain convinced that their descriptions of reality corresponded directly with what they describe. This word-event marriage is where two become one, and are indistinguishable. 'I call 'em as they are' is a view that says the conversation we have about faithful existence is prosecuted, without distortion, in discipleship, and the words that describe it. This realist view remains determinative for some sections of the church. The way we describe the world is the way it is.

2. I call 'em as I see 'em.

This possible view recognises the cultural limitation of all ways of seeing the world. 'I call 'em as I see 'em' acknowledges that it is my view of the world I declare, not *the* view of the world. There are other possible interpretations, as any umpire listening to enraged spectators well knows. The caller is declaring a commitment to his or her way of seeing the world.

Such a view acknowledges pluralism and makes space for divergent interpretations. This 'idealist' view of the world has shades of expression. What we seek to describe is significantly influenced by what we choose to affirm and grant attention. Here the confessional stance is clearly inescapable.

3. Until I call 'em they don't exist.

The third possible view, in philosophical terms a form of nominalism, suggests that within the context of the game it is our choice which makes the game possible. 'Until I call 'em they don't exist' gathers together those who wish to argue that all that we see, culture, art, science, religion, has no necessary existence, only a contingent existence dependent upon human creativity and choice.

At its crudest, nothing exists that we did not create in the realm of the non-physical world. It is our commitment, our creative energies, that make the game possible. Without our declaring what is there, nothing we see has a meaningful existence. Just as a ' strike' only exists as such in the game of baseball when it is named a 'strike', and then only has meaning in the wider context of the game, so too does language give life and meaning to all other 'games' in which we participate in ordered society.

In each of these three ways of viewing the world, the commitment declared is tied to assumptions about the way we are to seek meaning. Each of them has significant consequences for how we talk about

God and God's action within the created order. In a time when we cling to the wreckage of the ship which has carried generations through storms to the present chaos, how we understand what we are in significantly shapes how we seek to find an answer. In the end, the confessional stance we embrace determines what we see and what we can say.

For those who find the image of clinging to the wreckage real, the possibilities offered by the third confession above, while disturbing, may offer an exciting point of departure. When Paul was in a ship being driven by the storm to inevitable destruction, his advice to trust God was all sufficient.

But what does it mean to trust God? Today, we feel compelled to discover new ways of telling what trusting God means in a time of the 'death of God'. Naming the situation we are in is a necessary first step. Being aware as far as we can about other possible interpretations follows as a corrective to a narrow, one channel view of reality.

In that task, narrative inquiry can be the means of entering a new place, of changing our perceptions in ways that are gentle and freeing, of learning again of God's gracious presence in that game we call life. We should trust ourselves to employ the freedom we have been given. To say to each other, out of the realm of creative imagination, 'until we call 'em they don't exist'. That is the promise and gift of narrative, that we can be co-creators of the worlds we inhabit, as we are called to be.

Chapter 14

Uluru journey

It has been suggested in a previous chapter that we live in an age of disenchantment, in the technical sense that mythical world-views are no longer regarded as viable currency. The original sense of myth as being 'at the heart of things' has disappeared in the belief that only concrete, factual descriptions of human life are real. Even within the frame of story itself, a disillusion with mythic world views can be conveyed. Two examples demonstrate this claim.

Climbing mountains

In their play *The Ascent of F6*, W. H. Auden and Christopher Isherwood sought to destroy the diseased romanticism associated with nationalist aspirations of the 1930s. [61] They chose the image of the conquering of a mountain to symbolise the evil outcome of nationalist self-glorification. The eighteenth century was a period of high romanticism. People climbed mountains and claimed that there was something innately spiritual about the experience. In taking risks in such a setting, the climber was lifted above the commonplace, in an heroic projection that spoke of the ineffable. This mood still prevailed in the early decades of this century

F6 was a mountain that stood on a boundary between two nations. Britain decided to claim it for strategic and symbolic reasons despite the cost involved, mainly because another nation sought to conquer it. A demon lived on its summit according to the tribes who lived at the foot of the mountain. The demon must be conquered if the mountain is to be won. The authors of *The Ascent of F6* named the demon as a Freudian mother complex, associated not with the tragic heroes' own mother, although that image is strong, but the 'mother country' Great Britain.

Here was the source of destruction in the myths of empire and glory that brought death upon the four climbers who sought to claim the mountain for Britain. *The Ascent of F6*, the play, set out to demolish the illusion of nobility and the dream of empire that sustained it. Behind the surface meaning of the play was a sustained attack on its mythological ground and the world view that rose from it.

In 1970, Donald Bartheme wrote a story titled *The Glass Mountain*, which is included in the *Oxford Book of Modern Fairy Tales*. [62] It is an ugly and cynical story. The mountain is a skyscraper. Mixing mythical imagery with a contemporary urban landscape, filled with foul mouthed, abusive spectators, Bartheme has a climber scale the skyscraper and successfully reach the top. Above awaits a beautiful princess.

When the climber has almost reached the top, as legend demands, an eagle appears. The climber grasps its claws and is carried over the top to float above the glittering palace. Drawing a small knife from his belt, the climber cuts off the feet of the eagle and drops lightly into the palace. The story concludes in this way.

97. I approached the symbol with its layers of meaning,
    but when I touched it I found only a beautiful princess.
98. I threw the beautiful princess headlong down the
    mountain to my acquaintances.
99. Who could be relied upon to deal with her?
100. Nor are eagles plausible, not at all, not for a moment.

The *Glass Mountain* shares with *The Ascent of F6* a heavy cynicism, an anti-feminine sentiment, and a preoccupation with violence and death. Both stories pronounce the end of mythological validity in a world of harsh realism. There is also an echo of the same conclusion in A.N. Wilson's commendation of Karen Armstrong's book *A History of God*. [63]

This is the most fascinating and learned survey of the biggest goose chase in history - the quest for God.

There is a deep rift in much of the literature of the middle to late twentieth century which separates contemporary visions of human destiny from that which went before. Futility and meaninglessness predominate. For many, the final word is nihilism, the last state despair. We wait, unable to speak or move, for Godot.

Anyone in this kind of climate who seeks to awaken interest in narrative-symbolic themes is swimming against the tide. To employ as a root metaphor, the pilgrimage to a mountain, is to be doubly confounded. In a time when the death of God is felt as an existential absence, to seek for renewal of faith through narrative exploration is to place oneself on the other side of the divide, in a time which has passed and can be taken seriously no more.

But imagine for a moment that a case can be made for such an enterprise, as a religious pilgrimage. Narrative-symbolic language is the kind of language that conveys an event. It is the impact of the actions of people upon us that we are asked to engage. Theology in its systematic sense is secondary language which is concerned with the interpretation of events. Clearly there is a necessary relationship between primary and secondary language, but they are not the same and cannot be mistaken for each other.

Or, to say the same thing the other way around, a proper distinction needs to be made so that each form of discourse can do its own work. Where theological reflection does its work best is in turning us back again to the primary event of which it speaks and gives coherent interpretation. It is a different language from the language of religious experience and should not be seen as prior to that upon which it reflects.[64]

Religious language, as distinct from theological language, is always in direct engagement with the four horsemen of our time - meaninglessness, freedom, alienation and death. Here the motifs central to the human predicament are unveiled, and meaning, responsibility, community and life are brought as response to the threats detailed above to human purpose. To offer a hope-filled vision is to begin again from the realm of event, vivid direct experience, in order that the language of theological reflection itself become more immediate and communicative.

There are two concerns here. One is to make a Christian interpretation of life possible. The other arises from the experience of being unmoved by traditional theological statements, and being distanced from our own reality by the language employed. There is no escape from this dilemma concerning language and meaning for all language presupposes a mythology. Even so, some attempt must be made to recover a narrative ground that gives unity to individual and community identity. The unity spoken of here arises from a narrative quest that seeks a renewed vision of our shared journey, and gives us words which communicate directly the commitment involved.

Uluru Journey

In the first eleven chapters of this book, an attempt was made to illustrate how use could be made of narrative to further theological inquiry. Any description of the ingredients of that narrative immediately fall under the prohibition mentioned above of changing the nature of 'story' by explanation. As we progress from direct experience to reflective meditation and then analysis, a transformation occurs. The final outcome, if followed through, would be to turn us back again to action. C. S. Lewis argued this way. 'I am a rationalist. For me, reason is the natural organ of truth, but imagination is the organ of meaning. Imagination, producing new metaphors or revivifying old, is not the cause of truth, but its condition.' [65]

Elsewhere I have commented on this viewpoint in the following manner:

> It was the contention of Lewis that the symbolic realm in which meaning resides (and which is also the kingdom of faith) is not rationally but imaginatively understood. Only when concepts have been turned into images do they appear real to the human mind. This suggests a process in which images rising from experience are formed into concepts which are then transmuted back into images in order to communicate their truth. Meaning is therefore an integration of both reason and imagination in which reason is guided not by its own structural logic but that which comes co-operatively from the domain of imagination.'[66]

In this light, some discussion of Uluru Journey might profitably be undertaken, with due attention to the different requirements of reading intuitively, reflectively, analytically and theologically. We should heed the warning of Ruben Alves:

> Did you understand the story?
> I hope not...
> If you did it is because you have succeeded in digesting it.
> But stories are like poems; they are not to be understood.
> Something which is understood is never repeated.
> Understanding exhausts the word. It leaves the word empty with nothing left to be said. Once the word is understood it is reduced to silence.
> But a story is like a sonata, a love embrace, a poem, a sunset: we want them to be repeated, because their savour is inexhaustible.' [67]

The unreal ground of Uluru Journey

Metaphor

The root metaphor of *Uluru Journey* is that of a quest, and a particular kind of journey, a pilgrimage. So central to our conscious existence is the idea of journey that everyday conversation is scarcely possible without it. For journey is an icon of time, place, circumstance and purpose. When it is conceived of as a pilgrimage, then the spiritual dimension is declared to be central to its intent.

Pilgrimage

To give structure to the pilgrimage to Uluru, the pattern of *Canterbury Tales* was used. Just as in Chaucer's time, when people went regularly on a pilgrimage for religious purposes, so here in a minibus a group of people set out on a religious quest. There are differences. In Chaucer's story his pilgrims set out for a cathedral where the shrine of Thomas A'Beckett was located. All is defined and manifest, the purpose of the journey clear and specific.

In *Uluru Journey*, there is no cathedral, for cathedrals do not function as luminous centres of devotion for Australians, with or without the bones of martyrs. The focus instead is an arkose monolith, which means that all is not defined or manifest. The purpose of the journey is not entirely clear and not entirely specific in the same way. A vision of a God-centred universe is a hard idea to make specific in the wide expanses of the Australian outback although its possibility is redolent in every red-coloured vista and bounding kangaroo.

Image

If the root metaphor is a journey, its central image is a mountain. Not just any mountain. More truly a monolith. The largest monolith on earth, and the symbol for a nation of many people. A singularity, for no comparisons are possible with what the Rock means in the Australian psyche.

Its uniqueness makes it a proper object of any pilgrimage. Its ancient mantle of myth clings to it so that the sense of the mysterious is always present. It is not a cathedral but it is there for everyone. So Uluru is a fitting place to visit for those who go on pilgrimage, who travel to fulfil the heart's desire.

The place

The location of Uluru in a desert also calls up mythological images. One of them is Jesus in the desert wrestling with his destiny and tempted by many desirable but illusory options. The solitude of the lonely vastness, the sense of endless space, the brilliance of the stars, all of these and many more strip away pretence and deception. The outcome of intimacy and frankness which characterises the stories testifies to the effect of travelling in a desert. To reach the mountain, one must pass for a long time through the desert. There is a stark reality about the setting that speaks to our experience of spiritual struggle.

The People

Each traveller is an ordinary person by the usual standards of such judgments. They express a diversity of socio-economic, cultural and religious background. There is age and gender difference. There is a wide variance in attainment of formal educational qualifications and life experience. Like Katherine Porter's *The Ship of Fools*, [68] where the

147

ship functions as a metaphor for society, so here, as in Chaucer's work, the ordinariness and diversity speaks of Australian society and its hopes and aspirations, even of its destiny.

Limit situations
Each of the story-tellers in their recital touch on the four kinds of threats to purpose and meaning which are the companions on every journey. The limit situations of meaninglessness, freedom, alienation and death are woven through the narrative so that the reader can pursue these threads as another level of interpretation.

Levels of Myth
The four levels associated with every myth - cosmological, religious, psychological and sociological - are also present, running as a framework throughout the stories told. In a myth - these dimensions exist in an unbroken harmony. The predicament of our time - to hold all four dimensions together in unity - is clearly present. What seems inescapable are the human dilemmas. They represent the fundamental ground of narrative and identify the human hunger for resolution of the mystery of existence.

Orientation
There is another intended layer of meaning. The story-tellers hold positions on a philosophical spectrum from naive realism (the world is as it is) through idealism to a nominalist position (the world is what I create) with the viewpoint appropriate to each philosophical stance expressed through the four dimensions of myth.

Affects
Each of the pilgrims holds a view of the Divine, some overtly, some tacitly, that are detailed in most studies of the phenomenology of religion. These include in no particular order, so as not to spoil the fun, of awe, wonder, apprehension of mystery, trust, acceptance, commitment, love and joy, ethical structure, primal order, harmony, giftedness, and hunger for transcendence. The thirteen options listed above allow for some pairing of possibilities since not even a literary device can keep all of the borders discrete.

The Mountain
At the heart is the central image of Uluru which can function in a number of ways as a symbol of the Divine. Only one of the pilgrims names the God who speaks to him from the mountain and that in explicitly Christian terms. The intention here is to underline that the ineffable can be encountered but not described. People have many ways of sharing their sense of the Other which cannot be confined to one linguistic tradition. Language here is a poor medium which explains why, at appropriate moments, ritual actions are included that

without being named, point to other levels of meaning and shared experience across time and across cultures.

Thresholds
There is space also to reflect on the thresholds that confront the travellers and the choices that face them. Such choices require a step beyond known territory into the uncharted and uncertain. There are thresholds to be crossed in every journey, some of which are consciously recognised, some of which are not. Where a liminal situation confronts us the breakdown of the known can be the occasion of new birth.

Question and Answer
If the visit to Uluru is viewed as similar in kind to those who came to the Oracle at Delphi with a question on their lips, then each of the travellers brought a question Each received an answer although it may not be evident to them that it is so. Always, engagement with the Divine involves ambiguity, even if it is as vivid as the experience of travellers on the Emmaus road.[69]

Is the figure who joins us on the road actually flesh and bones, or that inner teacher, that prods us to recall what we know and offers the invitation to trust it. There is always in narrative engagement the possibility of imaginative identification which can lead us along paths and invite us into dialogues that transform all that we know.

Story
More significantly perhaps is the intertwining of personal story, community story, tribal-national story and universal story. It is difficult to draw the lines and to point with confidence to separation between these levels of story. In its original sense, myth meant to be centred. To be at the heart of things, as the Zen masters tell us, is also to be at the edge, for outside and inside are one when viewed with the eye of faith.

Issues
At a more prosaic level, the travellers present contemporary debates concerning Aboriginal cultural integrity, ethnic identity, multi-culturalism, feminism, the debate between science and religion, death and dying, the viability of belief in a materialist world, socio-economic disadvantage and even ecology. These issues are tied up with national identity and the meaning of the word 'Australian'.

The question of whether Uluru with all of its mythological overtones can function as a unifying symbol in the land which almost became 'The Land of the Holy Spirit' is an open one.[70] Does the attempt to garner our shared experience as dwellers in the land of Australia have any future reality? If it is the story we tell that binds us together, and we are in a time when we need a new story, then perhaps it is worth trying, however inadequate the outcome, to sing a new song and tell a new story, whose aim is universality and inclusiveness.

In this, we must turn to our artists and poets and storytellers. And since such an impulse to unity must arise from the lives of the people, it is their stories that need to be heard. Stories of the neglected, the marginalised, the silenced, the young and old, as well as those who hold the high ground and wield the instruments of power, should have equal honour when guests are gathered to the feast.

Unexpected outcomes

There are levels to the story that cannot be named, or even anticipated. All stories have a life of their own, and, once set free, fly where they will and come home to rest in the most unlikely places, carrying unexpected messages containing unanticipated good news. There is no way that the end can be anticipated when such good news is free in the world to do its work.

The one thing needful

In a time when the old has not entirely passed away and the new has not yet fully come, in a time between past present and future present, we do what faithful people have always done. We trust that we shall find a highway in the desert. Until then, we do what we know is sustaining of our life and its journey. We break bread. We drink wine. And we tell our stories.

Joseph Campbell echoes the One who said the gift of such a process is abundant life:

> People say that what we're all seeking is a meaning in life. I don't think that's what we're really seeking. I think that what we're seeking is an experience of being alive, so that our life experiences on the purely physical plane will have resonances within our own innermost being and reality, so that we actually feel the rapture of being alive.[71]

The debate with revelation

The strongest resistance to this open stance comes from those who hold a revelational theology which asserts that truth is given to experience, not derived from it. What the church does is faithfully protect the integrity of that which was entrusted to the Apostles, and which has been zealously proclaimed and strenuously protected from error down to the present time. Jesus is the same, yesterday, today and forever. Epiphanies in our time are not to be expected. What is to be revealed has been revealed and will remain intact and without remainder for all time. The task of the church is to continue faithful to what has been given and to resist all temptations that incite relevance, change, and trendiness.

Much could be said by way of response. There are many cultured despisers who turn away from a church that will not hear that what is offered has no meaning for them. If there is rejection, it is of a church which will not respond to the call to leave all that has been secured, in order to find new forms of being God's people, for the sake of those who are losing their story and with it a secure identity of who they are. We are about the recovery of tradition, not its rejection.

We can agree that no one can discover God. That would be to turn God into an object, and theology has always affirmed that God is eternally subject. But we cannot stay in Egypt and fulfil our destiny. We must say yes, and leaving safe ways behind, risk ourselves in new ways.

There are those who hear this call. And others who cannot, because they believe they are commanded to stay faithful to what is known. This book is written for travellers, for pilgrims, for those who look for a city that is to come, who do not find their heart's ease in what is to hand: people who go on knocking on doors, people who go on seeking, sustained by the promise that if they seek they will find, people who go on asking for they believe they will receive. The end of this striving is not just personal fulfilment, but a renewed social order, a rule of justice, a nation made one by a common story and a common vision. All of us need to make our journey to Uluru in order to find what we must do. The way, unavoidably, is through the desert.

A theological ground for narrative consciousness

By way of conclusion, some central affirmations can be made that draw the conversation to a close.

- Human beings need to tell a story in which meaning and primary heroism give direction to the life we live. By story we create, appropriate, and celebrate the world.
- Buried in the story our lives tell is a struggle to live a life which celebrates some fundamental integrity and truth.
- It is not possible to do something well unless we can imagine or envision what it is that we seek to make manifest.
- In seeking to develop our own narrative consciousness, we are struggling not only to be present to ourselves, our own time and circumstances and its particular tasks, but also to create a story that unveils a fundamental confession about who we are and what we believe.
- That story is personal, communal and God-shaped. It is a story mutually created, recognised and told. In such a case, it has the status of myth.
- The context in which we seek to incarnate this story is the source of its true meaning and value. The human action that defines a

151

story is a declaration of a basic faith. We are seeking and seek to live by, the stories that embody our basic faith.

- The journey into meaning/righteousness/justice, the development of a narrative consciousness, needs to be guided by a symbol system that is theologically sensitive since the symbolic is rooted in the psychic depths of the personality. There is a constant need to mediate our engagement by primary symbols and root metaphors about faith and its demand. We live out of imagination, and are called into being by the anticipatory trajectories of story and narrative.
- Images, stories, ritual actions, gestures, provide models and motives for the decisions and actions that shape our lives.
- What we intend by our human story is a comprehensive celebration since its end is God. The most appropriate guide of that story given in our images, paradigms, models and goals, lies in our meditative reflection on the life, death and resurrection of Jesus Christ.
- All of this can be articulated, however inadequately, by the story/ies we tell, through narrative consciousness, that has its particular guiding expression in 'aliveness'. The gift is more life.

Three propositions can be made:

- Persons communicate and relate to each other by the stories they tell.
- There can be no community life, no consensus and thus no common action without participation in a common understanding of the meaning of a common story, and without a common commitment to that story's value.
- The Jesus story is the foundation for the story of the community of faith, in all of its breathtaking wonder and unending invitation.

The story of the simple Rabbi

One final story concludes the exploration of the previous pages.

There was once a Rabbi who was a simple, cheerful and holy man, who guided his disciples in ways that would lead them to be simple, cheerful and holy. But one day they complained. 'Rabbi, why do you not sound more learned, share great ideas and construct great theories like the other Rabbis do? Can't you do anything but speak with simple words like an old grandmother, and tell tales? The good Rabbi smiled and began to speak.
'One day, the nettles asked the rosebush, "Mother Rosebush teach us your secret. How do you make a rose?" The

rosebush answered, "My secret is simple. All winter long I work the soil patiently, trustfully, lovingly and have only one thing in mind; the rose. The rains lash me, the wind strips my leaves, the snows crush me but I have only one thing in mind; the rose. That, Sister Nettles, is my secret."

'We don't understand Master' said the disciples.

The Rabbi laughed. 'I don't understand very well myself. But I think I want to say something like this. When I have an idea, I work it for a long time, silently, patiently, trustfully, lovingly. And when I speak, and here is the mystery, when I open my mouth, the idea comes out as a tale'.

The Rabbi laughed again. 'We humans call it a tale', he said, 'the rosebush calls it a rose.' [72]

Appendix

Some readers of this book may be interested in developing learning-teaching events within which story and narrative are used as a means of exploring faith and its implications for daily life. The following material has been helpful in devising settings and providing direction for the planning of a learning-teaching event. This appendix is provided as a possible guide to the setting up of small group encounters in local settings.

A collaborative planning process has proved to be more productive of genuine participation when a learning-teaching event is being developed. The outcomes of such events have been significant and enduring for participants, and the rewards for risking new ventures in exploring faith great. One key has been thorough planning which the following guidelines make possible.

Guidelines and reflection on a learning-teaching event

1. Before

1.1 Design

Is the design of the learning-teaching event clear?
Is the overall goal and objectives of each session defined?
Are learning-teaching activities identified and appropriate?
Are resources appropriate, plentiful and available?

1.2 Environment

Has attention been given to the learning-teaching environment?
Is teaching space appropriate to what is planned?
Is the environment free of competing attractions?
Are participants comfortable, warm and at ease?
Are teaching aids/resources ready and prepared for use?

1.3 Participants

Are participants well informed about what is to happen?
Have participants been positively motivated to engage in the learning process?
Has attention been given to the needs of the age group, their past experience of learning, and their readiness for the learning-teaching event?

2. During

2.1 Stories
Were the stories used suitable, of high quality, well understood?
Were the stories presented well and in a professional manner?
Were directions clear?
Were questions precise and appropriate?

2.2 Leader
Was the leader at ease in charge of the material and the process of the teaching event?
Were instructions given in a clear, easily heard and understood manner?
Did the leader show confidence and make the learning group feel relaxed and motivated?
Were questions or difficulties handled in a calm and competent way?
Were participants listened to by the leader?

2.3 Beginning and Ending
Was the opening of the learning-teaching event precise and well handled?
Were people welcomed and expectations checked?
Were overall directions given and questions well answered?
Were directions about time availability and time use given?
Was there a chance for a summing up?
Was there a definite closure to the learning-teaching event?
What mechanisms were used to call forth and to reinforce learning?
Was the role of the leader clear in opening, running and closing the learning-teaching event?

3. After
Was there a general air of satisfaction among participants?
Were goals achieved, objectives attained?
Was the use of story well integrated, systematic and sustained throughout the learning-teaching event?
Was inclusive language used and attention given to the participation of all group members?
Did people enjoy themselves?
Was the leader able to deal with disruptive or negative responses creatively?

Final reflection
What was done well?
What could have been done better?
What changes for future events should be made?

Select Bibliography

Alves, Ruben. *The poet, the warrior, the prophet.* The Edward Cadbury Lectures, SCM Press London/Trinity Press International, Philadelphia, 1990.

Arcodia, Charles. *Stories for sharing.* E. J. Dwyer, Newtown, NSW, 1991.

Armstrong, Karen. *A History of God.* Mandarin, London, 1993.

Auden, W. H. and Isherwood, Christopher. *The ascent of F6.* Faber & Faber, London, 1953.

Beane, Wendell C. & Doty, William G. (Eds) *Myths, rites, symbols.* A Mircea Eliade Reader, Vol 1/11, Harper Torchbacks, N.Y. 1975.

Berman, Morris. *Coming to our senses.* Bantam (New Age) Books, New York, Toronto, London, 1989.

—*The reenchantment of the world.* Bantam Books, Toronto, New York, London, Sydney, 1984.

Bernanos, Georges. *The diary of a country priest.* Carroll-Graf, New York, 1993.

Bettelheim, Bruno. *The uses of enchantment: the meaning and importance of fairy tales.* Alfred A. Knopf, New York, 1976.

Berry, Thomas. *The dream of the earth.* Sierra Club, San Francisco, 1988.

Bonnefoy, Yves (compiled by). *Mythologies.* 2 Vols., trans. Wendy Doniger, University of Chicago Press, Chicago & London, 1991.

Boys, Mary C. *Educating in faith, maps and visions.* Harper and Row, San Francisco, 1989

Bradbury, Ray. *The golden apples of the sun.* Graftan, London, 1977.

Burton, Richard. (trans.) *The book of the thousand and one nights.* A selection by P. H. Newby, Arthur Barker Ltd., London, 1958.

Campbell, Joseph. *The masks of God: creative mythology.* Penguin Books, New York, 1976.

—*The power of myth* with Bill Moyers. Doubleday, New York, 1988.

Capra, Fritjof. *The tao of physics.* Flamingo Fontana Paperbacks, London, 1976.

Casper, Walter. *The God of Jesus Christ.* SCM Press, London, 1984.

Charlesworth, Max et al. (Ed.) *Religion in Aboriginal Australia: an anthology.* University of Queensland Press, St Lucia, 1984.

Chatwin, Bruce. *The songlines.* Picador Pan Books, London, 1987.

Chaucer, Geoffrey. *The Canterbury Tales.* An illustrated selection rendered into modern English by Nevill Coghill, Penguin Books/Allen Lane, London, 1977.

Clark, Manning. *A History of Australia.* Vol. 1. Melbourne University Press, Melbourne, 1977.

Coles, Robert. *The call of stories: Teaching and the moral imagination.* Houghton Mifflin, Boston, 1989.

Cotterell, Arthur. *The Macmillan illustrated encyclopedia of myths and legends.* Macmillan Publishing Co., New York, 1989.

Cox, Philip. *Yulara.* Panda Books, McMahons Point, 1986.

Cupitt, Don. *Life lines.* SCM Press, London 1986.

—*What is a story?* SCM Press, London, 1991.

—*The longlegged fly.* SCM Press, London, 1987.

—*The sea of faith.* SCM Press, London, 1994.

Dante. *Portraits of greatness.* Elite Publishing Corporation, New York, 1967.

Das, Surya. *The snow lions turquoise mane, Wisdom tales from Tibet.* Harper, San Francisco, 1992.

Davies, Paul. *The mind of God. Science and the search for ultimate meaning.* Penguin Books, Australia Ltd., 1992.

—*The cosmic blueprint.* Heinemann, London, 1988.

de Mello, Anthony. *The song of the bird.* Gujarat Sahitya Prakash Anand, India, 1982.

Donaldson, Stephen. *Daughter of regals and other tales.* William Collins Sons & Co., London, 1984.

Dowling, Terry. *Rhynossoros.* Aphelion Press, North Adelaide, 1990.

Driver, Tom. *The magic of ritual. Our need for liberating rites that transform our lives and our communities.* Harper, San Francisco, 1991.

Eliot, T. S. *The complete poems and plays.* Faber & Faber, London, 1969.

English, Peter B. *Storm over Uluru :The greatest hoax of all.* Veritas Publishing Co., Chitering, Qld. 1986.

Estes, Clarissa Pinkola. *Women who run with the wolves.* Rider, London, 1994.

Fox, Matthew. *The coming of the cosmic Christ.* Collins Dove, Melbourne, 1988.

Gardner, Howard. *Frames of mind. The theory of multiple intelligences.* Basic Books, New York, 1985.

Goodman, Nelson. *Languages of art: An approach to a theory of symbols.* Bobbs-Merrill, Indianapolis, 1968.

Grierson, Denham. *Conversations at the edges of the raft.* Collins Dove, Melbourne, 1993.

—*Transforming a people of God.* Joint Board of Christian Education, Melbourne, 1984.

Griffin, David R. (Ed.) *Sacred interconnections.* State University of New York Press, Albany, 1990.

Gregory, Bruce. *Inventing reality. Physics as language.* John Wiley & Sons, New York, 1990.

Hamerton-Kelly, Robert G. *Sacred violence. Paul's hermeneutic of the cross.* Fortress Press, Minneapolis, 1992.

Hammarskjold, Dag. *Markings.* trans. Leif Sjoberg & foreword W. H. Auden, Faber & Faber, London, 1964.

Harney, W.E. *Tales from the Aborigines*. Robert Hale Ltd., London, 1959.

—*The story of Ayers Rock*. A Bread and Cheese Club Production, Melbourne, 1957.

Harney, Bill/Elkin, A.P. *Songs of the songmen. Aboriginal myths retold.* Rigby,Adelaide. 1949.

Hawking, Stephen W. *A brief history of time, from the big bang to black holes.* Bantam Books, Toronto, 1992.

Hauerwas, Stanley and Jones, L. Gregory (Eds). *Why narrative? Readings in narrative theology.* William B. Eerdmans, Grand Rapids, Michigan, 1989.

Horton, David (Gen. Ed.). *The encyclopaedia of Aboriginal Australia.* Vol. 2. Aboriginal Studies Press for Australian Institute of Aboriginal and Torres Strait Islander Studies, Canberra,1994.

Kabukiwa, Robin and Grace, Patricia. *Wahine Toa: Women of Maori myth.* Collins, Auckland, 1984.

Kazantzakis, Nikos. *Report to Greco.* trans. P.A. Bien, Bruno Cassirer, Oxford, 1965.

—*The odyssey : A modern sequel.* trans. Kimon Friar, Secker & Warburg, London, 1959.

Kierkegaard, Soren. *Either/Or.* Vol. 1. Anchor Books, New York, 1959.

—*Fear and trembling and the sickness unto death.* trans. Walter Lowrie, Princeton University Press Paperback, Princeton, New Jersey, 1954.

Layton, Robert. *Uluru: An Aboriginal history of Ayers Rock.* Aboriginal Studies Press, Canberra, 1989.

McFague, Sallie. *Metaphorical theology. Models of God in religious language.* SCM Press, London, 1983.

McKenzie, Doug. *The Mango Tree Church. The Story of the Protestant Christian Church in Bali.* Boolarong Publications/Joint Board of Christian Education, Brisbane, 1988.

MacIntyre, Alasdair. *After virtue.* University of Notre Dame Press, Notre Dame, 1981.

Mack, Eric and Rudd, Richard. *The Rock.* Rigby, Adelaide, 1976.

Macquarrie, John. *In search of Deity.* SCM Press, London, 1984.

Miller, Donald. *Story and context. An introduction to Christian education.* Abingdon, Nashville, 1987.

Milton, Ralph. *The gift of story.* Wood Lake Press, Toronto, 1982.

Moore, Mary Elizabeth Mullino. *Teaching from the heart. Theology and educational method.* Fortress Press, Minneapolis, 1991.

Moran, Gabriel. *Religious education as a second language.* Religious Education Press, Birmingham, Alabama, 1989.

Mountford, Charles P. *Ayers Rock. Its people, their beliefs and their art.* Angus & Robertson, Sydney, 1965.

Neidjie, Bill. *Kakadu man.* Mybrood P/L Inc. NSW, Allan Fox & Associates, 1985.

Ollier, C.D. *Geology of Ayers Rock*. Northern Territory Reserves Board, undated.

Polkinghorne, Donald E. *Narrative knowing and the human sciences*. Albany State University of New York Press, New York, 1988.

Porter, Katherine. *The ship of fools*. Secker & Warburg, London, 1974.

Poulter, Jim. *The secret of dreaming*. Red Hen, Templestowe, 1988.

Reanney, Darryl. *The death of forever; A new future for human consciousness*, Longman Cheshire, South Melbourne, 1991.

Reed, A.W. *Aboriginal myths. Tales of the Dreamtime*. Reed Books, Balgowlah, 1978.

Shea, John. *Stories of God. An authorized biography*. Thomas More Press, Chicago, 1978.

Schwarz-Bart, Andre. *The last of the just*. Minerva Paperback, London, 1992.

Song, C. S. *Tell us our names : Story theology from an Asian perspective*. Orbis Books, Maryknoll, New York, 1984.

—*The tears of Lady Ming*. Orbis Books, Maryknoll, New York, 1981.

Strehlow, T. G. H. *Central Australian religion*. Australian Association for the Study of Religion, Special Studies in Religion Series, Vol. 2. Adelaide, 1978.

—*Personal monototemism in a polytotemic community*. Australian Association for the Study of Religions No. 2, Flinders University Press, Bedford Park, South Australia, 1978.

Stroup, George W. *The promise of narrative theology*. John Knox, Atlanta, 1981.

Swimme, Brian. *The universe is a green dragon*. Bear & Co., Sante Fe, New Mexico, 1984.

Talbot, Michael. *The holographic universe*. Harper Collins, New York, 1991.

Theophane the Monk. *Tales of a magic monastery*. Crossroad, New York, 1992.

Tracy, David. *The analogical imagination: Christian theology and the culture of pluralism*. Crossroad, New York, 1981.

Van Buren, Paul M. *The secular meaning of the gospel*. SCM Press, London, 1963.

Wallace, Phyl and Noel. *Killing me softly. The destruction of a heritage*. Thomas Nelson (Australia), Melbourne, 1977.

Weil, Simone. *Waiting for God*. Harper & Row, New York, 1973.

West, Morris. *The Ambassador*. Fontana/Collins, Glasgow, 1965.

Wicker, Brian. *The story shaped world: Fiction and metaphysics, some variations on a theme*. University of Notre Dame Athlone Press, London, 1975.

Wilder, Amos N. *Jesus' Parables and the war of myths. Essays on imagination in the scriptures*. Fortress Press, Philadelphia, 1982.

Wiesel, Elie. *Messengers of God : Biblical portraits and legends*. Random House, New York, 1976.

—*The fifth son*. trans. Marion Wiesel, Warner Books, New York, 1985.

Worms, Ernest Ailred. *Australian Aboriginal religions*. Spectrum for Nelen Yubu Missiological Unit, Richmond,Vic., 1986.

Zukav, Gary. *The dancing Wu Li masters* . Flamingo Fontana Paperbacks, London, 1986.

Articles

Bartheme, Donald. 'The Glass Mountain' in *The Oxford book of modern fairy tales*. (Ed.) Alison Lurie, Oxford University Press, Oxford, 1993.

Bruner, Jerome. 'Narrative and Paradigmatic Modes of Thought' in *Learning and teaching the ways of knowing*. (Ed.) Elliot Eisner, Chicago Uni. of Chicago Press, 1985. 84th Yearbook National Society for the Study of Education.

Connelly, F. Michael & Clandinin D. Jean. 'Stories of experience and narrative inquiry'. *Educational Research* No. 5. June-July 1990.

Hunt, Rex. *'Please tell us your stories'* : *Re-imagining the 'poetic' in religious communication*. Paper presented to the Third Christianity and Communication Conference, 'Faith, story and community', June 1993, Regent University, Virginia Beach, Virginia, USA.

Lane, Belden G. 'Rabbinical Stories: A Primer in Theological Method' in *The Christian Century*. December 16, 1981.

Lewis, C. S. 'Bluspels and Flalansferes' in *Rehabilitations*. Oxford Press, London, 1939.

Westerhoff, John. 'Contemporary Spirituality : Revelation, myth and ritual' in *Aesthetic dimensions of religious education*. (Ed.) G. Durka & J. Smith. Paulist Press, New York, 1979.

Notes

1. Researching the history of Uluru is not an easy task. Authorities disagree. There are varying accounts of the myths and details within myths are not always consistent. No one, however diligent, can be sure that what they learn is either accurate, commonly accepted or in any way certainly true. The account recorded here will be disputed by some, although considerable effort was made to be as comprehensive and accurate as possible.
Material has been taken from many sources, and grateful acknowledgment is made of the contribution of many writers. Some of the most influential sources consulted include the following: Charles Mountford's book *Ayers Rock, its people, their beliefs and their art*. Richmond's *Ayers Rock in historical perspective*, C. D. Ollier's *Geology of Ayers Rock* and particularly *The Rock*, by Eric Mack and Richard Rudd. *Aboriginal myths, tales of the Dreamtime*, by A. W. Reed, *Australian Aboriginal religions* by Ernest Worms and *The encyclopaedia of Aboriginal Australia, Volume 2*, were also helpful. T. G. H. Strehlow's *Personal monototemism in a polytotemic community* is a significant resource.
Reference was made to *Yulara*, by Philip Cox, as well as the writings of W. E. Harney, despite the current scepticism held by scholars concerning the accuracy of his perceptions of Aboriginal legends and society. The geological description quoted in the text come from one of his early publications in 1957, *The story of Ayers Rock* (p. 9). Although Harney was not a geologist, he quotes geologists in this passage. Reference to Ollier, and Ollier and Tuddenham, confirms this early account. *Uluru: an Aboriginal history of Ayers Rock*, by Robert Layton, is an important reference.
I received considerable help from librarians at Nungalinya College, the University of Darwin and its collection of Aboriginal literature housed in the Djarra Djagamirri Room, the Nevil Shute memorial library in Alice Springs, the Institute for Aboriginal Development and in visiting the Strehlow museum, also in Alice Springs. Full details of the above sources are included in the bibliography.
In order to keep footnotes to a minimum, particular reference to sources has been sparsely used in the text. Acknowledgement, however, is made of the contribution of the above material to what has been included in the first chapter. There are others who might also be acknowledged, but the task of identifying the influence of all sources is complex, and not always a matter of conscious awareness. Any omission, therefore, is unintentional and not an avoidance of proper recognition of those who have contributed to what has been gathered, either by oral or written communication.

2. The dreaming story of Uluru as being a mud pile formed by child spirits playing has not been included in the text, although available in a number of collections of Aboriginal mythology. One version can be found in *Uluru: an Aboriginal history of Ayers Rock*, by Robert Layton, Aboriginal Studies Press, Canberra, 1989.

3. The reference is to *Canterbury Tales* by Geoffrey Chaucer written between 1387 and 1392. Chaucer describes a pilgrimage in which the pilgrims tell tales as they travel. There are many translations of Chaucer's classic. One simple translation, rendered into modern English, is that of Nevill Coghill published originally by Penguin Books, London. It is Coghill's translation that is used here, in the Allen Lane publication of 1977.

4. Ibid, p. 35. In *Canterbury Tales*, the observation is passed on a faithful priest, much loved, and approved by Chaucer.

5. Chatwin, Bruce, *The Songlines*, Picador Pan Books, London, 1987.

6. Poulter, Jim, *The Secret of Dreaming*, a children's book, published by Red Hen, 1988. In order to honour the original story, no attempt has been made to address the issue of exclusivist language. Here and elsewhere in the text, when quoting other writers, the original use of the male gender when both male and female are intended, has been left as written by the authors concerned. In the text of this book, however, every attempt has been made to use inclusive language.

7. In this monologue, I am heavily dependent upon the reminiscences of Bill Neidjie published in the book *Kadadu Man*, Mybrood Inc NSW, Allan Fox Associates, 1985.

8. The story told by Daniel Levi about his grandfather is fictitious, but it parallels the life story of Rosie Bruell, a survivior of Auschwitz and Bergen-Belsen. I learnt of her story on a visit to the Holocaust Museum where she sat and shared with me her memories of those years in bondage. Rosie, now in her seventies, like other survivors, dignifies the human race by her courage and compassion. 'We do not know why it happened, only how it happened.'. They tell their story that nothing like it will occur again.

9. Wallace, Phyl and Noel, *Killing me softly. The destruction of a heritage*. Thomas Nelson (Australia) Ltd, Melbourne, 1977.

10. The story that follows is dependent on *The last of the just*, by Andre Schwarz-Bart, Minerva, London, 1992. The quotation will be found on page 4 of *The last of the just*. No footnote or reference is provided. The legend of the just men is taken from Schwarz-Bart's account.

11. Ibid, p. 4.

12. Van Buren, Paul M., *The secular meaning of the Gospel*, SCM Press Ltd, London, 1963, p. 3. The original source of this story is from an article called 'Gods' originally published in *Proceedings of the Aristotelian society*, 1944. The form of it here is taken from *New essays in philosophical theology*, A. Flew and A. MacIntyre eds, SCM Press, London, 1955, p. 96.

13. The two stories included in this chapter, of Ketut and Wayan, had their origins in *Tales of a magic monastery* (Theophane the Monk, Crossroad, New York 1992). The ideas were taken by Doug McKenzie, re-shaped and re-written for a Balinese situation with considerable cultural veracity. In addition, McKenzie's book, *The Mango Tree Church. The Story of the*

Protestant Christian Church in Bali (The Joint Board of Christian Education, Boolarong Publications, Brisbane, 1988), has provided both information and interpretation for much else included in the text. Other ideas have come from conversation in Bali with members of the Balinese Protestant Church, which I visit occasionally to teach at clergy seminars.

The serious situation brought upon Bali by the tourist industry cannot be over-estimated. In this, Bali exists as a microcosm of the wider context of international tourism. Some experts are convinced that, given the present flood of tourists, the infrastructure and integrity of the island will be destroyed in twenty years. The human plague of tourists is decimating one of the most sensitive and beautiful cultures on the planet. The word SABDA can mean eternal word, or even, a religious utterance.

14. This sentence is taken from *Principles and practice of medicine*, Christopher R. W. Edwards, Ian A. D. Bouchier eds, 16th edition, Churchill Livingston, Edinburgh, London, Melbourne, 1991, p. 234.

15. Hammarskjold, Dag, *Markings*, (translated by Leif Sjoberg and W. H. Auden), Faber & Faber, London, 1964, pp. 67, 82, 87.

16. The story of *The Samurai and the tea master* is a traditional one. The version used here is an adaption from several sources. One of these is by Brian Cavanaugh in *Human development*, Vol. 8, No. 2, Summer 1987, p. 26.

17. *Markings*, p. 88.

18. The account given here of contemporary quantum physics is largely dependent upon Paul Davies and his various books that seek to inform lay people of the developments in science. Davies himself seems to take a stance to what he describes, somewhat akin to that of Colin Freeman. See his conclusion in *The mind of God*. The major reference, however, for the text here is not *The mind of God* or *God and the new physics*, but *The cosmic blueprint* (Heinemann, London, 1988). A description of the dilemma of Schrodinger's cat can be found on pp. 169-70. Another description of Erwin Schrodinger's paradox can be found in *Inventing reality* by Bruce Gregory (John Wiley & Sons Ltd., New York, 1990, p. 210).

19. Ibid.

20. Bradley, Ray, *The Golden Apples of the Sun*, Graftan, London, 1977, pp. 73ff.

21. Hawking, Stephen W., *A brief history of time*, Bantam Books, London, 1992, p. 185.

22. This story of Stephen Donaldson can be found in his book of short shories, *Daughter of regals and other tales*, Fontana Collins, Glasgow, 1988.

23. There are many variations of this story. This particular story in extended form can be found in *Women who run with the wolves*, by Clarissa Pinkola Estes, Rider, London, 1992, p. 120.

24. The story of Esau and Jacob can be found in the book of Genesis, from chapters 25 to 33.

25. Dante, *The divine comedy*: A poem in three parts, the Inferno, the Purgatorio and the Paradiso. In company with the poet Virgil, Dante wanders through Hell and Purgatory. In Purgatory, they ascend the mountain that has seven levels and reach the earthly paradise lost by Adam and Eve. See *Portraits of greatness - Dante*, Elite Publishing Corporation, New York 1967.

26. Kazantzakis, Nikos, *The Odyssey*, A Modern Sequel (trans. Kimon Friar), Secker & Warburg, London, 1959, p. 689.

27. *Markings*, p. 86.

28. The reference is to a football club which is one of sixteen teams included in the Australian Football League. Readers unfamiliar with Australian Rules football may be helped by the following information: Footscray Football Club has as its mascot a bulldog. Collingwood, another team, has a magpie as a symbol and is referred to often as the 'Pies by its supporters. Another team, Essendon, has the tag 'the Bombers' and St Kilda is 'the Saints' to its supporters. Later references in Archie's story will make sense against this background.

29. An original form of this story is told by Soren Kierkegaard in *Fear and trembling and the sickness until death* (trans. Walter Lowrie), Princeton University Press Paperback, Princeton, New Jersey, 1954, p. 187.

30. Many variations of this folk story exist and ascribing it to one particular source is risky. It has been rewritten for this telling.

31. West, Morris, *The Ambassador*, Fontana Collins, Glasgow, 1965, pp. 250-252.

32. Dowling, Terry, *Rynossoros*, Aphelion Press, North Adelaide, 1990, pp. 87, 89, 95.

33. Kierkegaard, Soren, *Either/Or*, Vol.1, Anchor Books, New York, 1959, p. 30.

34. *The Canterbury Tales*, p. 13.

35. Ibid, p. 14

36. *Writing a woman's life*, Carolyn G. Heilbrun, Norton, London, 1988, p. 37. 'Stories of Experience and Narrative Inquiry' in F. Michael Connelly and D. Jean Clandinin, *Educational Researcher*, No. 5 June-July 1990, p. 2.

38. *Wahine Toa women of Maori myth*, Robin Kabukiwa and Patricia Grace, Collins, Auckland, 1984.

39. Joseph Campbell, *The masks of God; creative mythology*, Penguin Books, New York, 1976, p. 609.

40. *The book of the thousand and one nights*, trans. Sir Richard Burton, A selection by P. H. Newby, Arthur Barker Limited, London, 1958.

41. Cupitt has developed this analysis steadily throughout a large body of work. See as examples, *Lifelines*, SCM Press, 1986, *The Longlegged Fly*, SCM Press, London, 1987, *The sea of faith*, revised edition SCM Press, London, 1994.

42. Stephen Hawking, *A brief history of time*, Bantam, Toronto, 1992, p. 185.

43. Simone Weil, *Waiting for God*, Harper and Row, New York, 1973, p. 32.

44. Thomas Berry, *The dream of the earth*, Sierra Club, San Francisco, 1988, p. 123.

45. Walter Casper, *The God of Jesus Christ*, SCM Press, London, 1984, p. 47-64.

46. Alasdair MacIntyre, *After virtue*, University of Notre Dame Press, Notre Dame, 1981, pp. 190-209.

47. Barbara Hardy, 'Towards a Poetics of Fiction: An Approach through Narrative', *Novel 2*, 1968, p. 5. Quoted in MacIntyre, *After virtue*, ibid.

48. John Westerhoff, 'Contemporary Spirituality: Revelation, myth and ritual', in Eds G. Durka and J. Smith, *Aesthetic dimensions of religious education*, Paulist Press, New York, 1979, pp. 20,23.

49. Brian Wicker, *The story shaped world : fiction and metaphysics, some variations on a theme*. Uni. of Notre Dame, Athlone Pr. London, 1975, p. 27.

50. Sally McFague, *Metaphorical theology, models of God in religious language*, SCM Press, London, 1983, p. 117.

51. Quoted by Belden G. Lane, 'Rabbinical stories: a primer on theological method' in *The Christian Century*, December 16, 1981, p. 1308.

52. Nikos Kazantzakis, *Report to Greco*, Trans P. A. Bien, Bruno Cassirer, Oxford, 1965, p. 234.

53. *Why narrative? Readings in narrative theology*. Eds Stanley, Hauerwas & L. Gregory Jones, William B. Eerdmans, Publishing Company, Grand Rapids, 1989, p. 5.

54. Don Cupitt, *What is a story*, SCM Press, London, 1991, p. 50.

55. T.S. Eliot agrees although for different reasons.

>   There is, it seems to us
>   At best, only a limited value
>   In the knowledge derived from experience

   Four Quartets in *The complete poems and plays*, Faber & Faber, London, 1969, p. 179.

56. Richard Niebuhr, *The meaning of revelation*, 'The Story of our Life', reprinted in *Why narrative*, p. 29.

57. Ibid, P. 29.

58. Ibid, p. 36.

59. *op. cit*, p. 167.

60. Ernest Gombrich in Nelson Goodman, *Languages of art: an approach to a theory of symbols*, Bobbs-Merrill, Indianapolis, 1968, pp. 7-8.

61. W. H. Auden and Christopher Isherwood, *The ascent of F6*, Faber and Faber, London, 1953.

62. 'The Glass Mountain' Donald Bartheme in *The Oxford book of modern fairy tales*, Ed. Alison Lurie. Oxford University Press, Oxford, 1993, pp. 367-371.

63. A. N. Wilson, *A history of God*, Karen Armstrong, Mandarin, London, 1993.

64. Sally McFague, op.cit. See a discussion of this distinction on pp. 119-120.

65. Bluspels and Flalansferes, in *Rehabilitations*, Oxford Press, London, 1939, p. 158.

66. *Transforming a People of God*, The Joint Board of Christian Education, Melbourne, 1984, p. 45.

67. Ruben Alves, *The poet, the warrior, the prophet*, The Edward Cadbury lectures, SCM Press/Trinity Press International, 1990, pp. 23-24.

68. Katherine Porter, *The ship of fools*, Secker and Warburg, London, 1974.

69. The Gospel according to St Luke, 24:13-35.

70. Manning Clark, *A history of Australia*, Vol. 1, Melbourne University Press, Melbourne, 1977, p. 15. On the Portuguese explorer Pedro Ferdinez de Quiros, Clark writes, 'He began to believe that he had been singled out by God as the vessel through whom the inhabitants of "Terra Australis" would be *Australia del Spiritu Santo* - a land dedicated to the Holy Spirit.' Had the Portuguese colonised Australia, its name would have been Australia del Espiritu Santo - the land of the Holy Spirit.

71. *The power of myth*, with Bill Moyers, Doubleday, New York, 1988, p. 5.

72. Adapted from Nikos Kazantzakis, *Report to Greco*, Bruno Cassirer, Oxford, 1961, pp. 474-475.